CONSTANCE
BAKER MOTLEY

T0288358

CONSTANCE
BAKER MOTLEY

*One Woman's Fight
for Civil Rights and
Equal Justice under Law*

Gary L. Ford Jr.

THE UNIVERSITY OF ALABAMA PRESS
Tuscaloosa

The University of Alabama Press
Tuscaloosa, Alabama 35487-0380
uapress.ua.edu

Hardcover edition published 2017.
Paperback edition published 2018.
eBook edition published 2017.

Inquiries about reproducing material from this work should be addressed to the
University of Alabama Press.

Typeface: Garamond

Cover image: Constance Baker Motley, January 25, 1966; Library of Congress
Prints and Photographs Division, *New York World-Telegram and Sun* Newspaper
Photograph Collection
Cover design: Todd Lape/Lape Designs

Author photo: Courtesy of Margot L. Jordan, International Photojournalist

Paperback ISBN: 978-0-8173-5933-1

A previous edition of this book has been catalogued by the Library of Congress
as follows:

Library of Congress Cataloging-in-Publication Data

Names: Ford, Gary L., Jr., 1977– author.
Title: Constance Baker Motley : one woman's fight for civil rights and equal
justice under law / Gary L. Ford Jr.
Description: Tuscaloosa, Alabama : The University of Alabama Press, 2017. |
Includes bibliographical references and index.
Identifiers: LCCN 2017001717| ISBN 9780817319571 (cloth : alk. paper) |
ISBN 9780817391447 (e book)
Subjects: LCSH: Motley, Constance Baker, 1921–2005. | Judges—New York
(State)—Biography. | Lawyers—New York (State)—Biography.
Classification: LCC KF373.M64 F67 2017 | DDC 347.73/14092 [B]—dc23
LC record available at https://lccn.loc.gov/2017001717

Contents

Acknowledgments

I have many people to thank for making this book a possibility. I start with Constance Royster (Connie), the namesake and niece of Judge Constance Baker Motley. When I was a child, Connie often invited my family to picnics at her home. I first met Judge Motley at one of those picnics. Later, when I was a young adult, Connie took me to visit Judge Motley at her country home in Connecticut. During that visit Judge Motley served chicken, mashed potatoes, green beans, and a "mile high" pie with ice cream. Before dinner Judge Motley talked with me about her civil rights work. She showed me photographs she had taken with Dr. Martin Luther King Jr. and the other civil rights activists she represented during the civil rights movement and scrapbooks filled with magazine clippings about the desegregation cases she had won and the people she had represented.

That African American history lesson motivated me to want to know more about the black experience in the United States, inspired me to major in African American history at Harvard University, and led me to select Judge Motley as the subject of my doctoral dissertation. It is with pleasure that I acknowledge Connie for planting the seed from which this book sprouted. It is also with pleasure and gratitude that I acknowledge Nancy L. Struna, the chairwoman of my dissertation committee, and John L. Caughey, Mary Corbin Sies, Sharon Harley, Psyche Williams-Forson, and Bernard Lafayette Jr. for the critical comments, recommendations, guidance, and support they provided as members of the committee.

I owe a special thanks to Joel Motley III, the son of Judge Motley, for graciously providing me with personal documents, books, audiotapes, and other material and for making arrangements for me to gain access to the papers of Judge

Motley that are stored but not yet catalogued at Columbia University. His graciousness and assistance were crucial in the completion of this book.

I owe a debt of gratitude to those who gave me personal interviews, spoke with me on the telephone, sent me written comments, permitted me to use their comments, or responded in other ways to my request for information about their experiences with Judge Motley. They are Maya Angelou, Derrick Bell, John Brittain, Bill Clinton, William T. Coleman Jr., Drew S. Days III, James Farmer, William Forbath, Ernest Green, Jack Greenberg, Charlayne Hunter-Gault, Lynn Huntley, Elaine Jones, Vernon E. Jordan Jr., Bernard Lafayette Jr., Carlotta Walls LaNier, Joel Motley III, James Nabrit, Charles J. Ogletree, Douglas Schoen, Laura Taylor Swain, Calvin Trillin, Wyatt Tee Walker, Juan Williams, Calvin Woods, Herbert Wright, and Andrew Young. I thank Marilyn Ford, my mother, for organizing the Life of Judge Constance Baker Motley Symposium in 2009, which helped to facilitate the primary research with those named here.

I am grateful to the University of Maryland and Quinnipiac University for providing the resources that allowed me to maintain a productive interchange of research, practical classroom application, and completion of my dissertation. I am also grateful to Lehman College of the City University of New York for providing the support that allowed me to complete the manuscript for this book and to Kenneth G. Standard, Nola Whiteman, Carl Turnipseed, and Joyce Turnipseed for the opportunities they created for me to present my work on Judge Motley.

Finally, I thank Dan Waterman and the University of Alabama Press for considering and accepting this book for publication.

CONSTANCE
BAKER MOTLEY

1

Clarifying and Correcting the Narratives of the Civil Rights Movement

As the lead lawyer either at trial or on appeal in dozens of public school desegregation cases throughout the South, [Constance Baker] Motley enforced *Brown* directly, attacking all of the delaying tactics of southern school systems. She also sued to desegregate transportation facilities, public housing, hospitals, motels, restaurants, parks, pools, libraries, and even golf courses.
—Richard Blum, "Constance Juanita Baker Motley,"
The Scribner Encyclopedia of American Lives

A key strategist of the civil rights movement, Constance Baker Motley waged the battle for equality in the courtroom and, with quiet courage and remarkable skill, won landmark victories that dismantled segregation in America. As a dedicated public servant and distinguished judge, she has broken down political, social, and professional barriers, and her pursuit of equal justice under law has widened the circle of opportunity in America.
—President Bill Clinton, awarding of the Presidential Citizen Medal, 2001

On a sunny day in 1959, five years after the US Supreme Court decision in *Brown v. Board of Education*, four lawyers—one of them an articulate, confident, well-dressed, and statuesque black woman—triumphantly walked out of the District Court for the Northern District of Georgia.[1] They had just won the case to desegregate public schools in Atlanta. The National Association for the Advancement of Colored People (NAACP) had filed the lawsuit on behalf of ten black parents in Atlanta a year earlier, in 1958. The parents were seeking admission of their children into the all-white Atlanta public schools. The separate all-black schools that their children attended were dilapidated and lacked books and other basic materials required to provide a quality education.

Judge Frank A. Hooper of the Georgia district court had issued the ruling declaring the racially segregated schools unconstitutional. He did not have the power to force integration, but he did have the power to order the schools to desegregate. Judge Hooper exercised that power and ordered Atlanta's school board to come up with a plan to end the dual system and to desegregate the schools.

Constance Baker Motley (1921–2005), the *only* female attorney at the NAACP Legal Defense and Educational Fund (known as the LDF) and the *only* woman who argued desegregation cases in court during most of the civil rights movement from 1946 to 1964, had the honor of being the lead counsel in the case. It was not her first significant legal victory. She was the legal strategist and trial counsel described as the LDF's "field general." By all accounts a gifted litigator, she was the person who was assigned and won many of the most difficult and important desegregation cases in the civil rights movement during the second half of the twentieth century.

The civil rights movement can be conceptualized as part of a movement for human rights and the struggle of disadvantaged and excluded groups against racism, sexism, and other inequalities as well as the struggle to attain social justice and inclusion in society. Other political and social movements—including the antiwar, feminist, LGBT (lesbian, gay, bisexual, and transgender), new immigrant, disability, environmental, and student movements—were inspired and galvanized by the black challenge to racism and discrimination. Susan Hartmann has argued that the black struggle for equality in the 1960s provided the model and inspiration for the other groups, which derived their ideologies, tactics, and legislative agenda from the civil rights example.[2]

The civil rights movement was made up of many smaller movements and campaigns to end official racial segregation and discrimination. It was not confined to the South; campaigns were waged in the North, East, and Midwest and in major cities and small rural areas across the United States. When most people think about the civil rights movement, they think about the national aspect, but it was the local grassroots activity that served as the backbone of the movement.

The struggle for equality extended beyond a challenge to segregation. It also focused on the disparity in economic opportunities, consumer credit, welfare rights, health care, and all aspects of social and political activities. The social movement spread over more than two decades. Civil rights campaigns were continuous struggles that began before *Brown* and continued after the assassination of Dr. Martin Luther King Jr. in Memphis in 1968.

Two of the more effective and complementary strategies employed by blacks in the civil rights movement were nonviolent protest and court action. Nonviolent protest involved the mobilization of blacks to participate in mass demonstrations to end official racial segregation and discrimination, achieve equality, and bring about social and political change. It was made up of many movements and grassroots campaigns. Recent feminist scholarly work demonstrates that although many of the movements and campaigns were primarily organized, led, and sustained by black female activists, charismatic men were given most of the credit for being the change agents and leaders of the civil rights movement.[3]

Court action, the second strategy employed in the movement, involved a legal challenge to de jure segregation policies and practices—to dismantle Jim Crow and to overturn the Supreme Court decision in *Plessy v. Ferguson*, the case that sanctioned racial segregation in American society and mandated "separate but equal" public accommodations.[4] Assistance in achieving the goals and objectives of the legal challenge came from the NAACP and its legal arm, the LDF. The organization used litigation to eradicate the Jim Crow system and to achieve social and political change.

The LDF led the battle in the courts and won crucial civil rights cases. It challenged segregation and inequality in education, public accommodations, transportation, employment, housing, and voting rights. Protest action and subsequent legal challenges led to social and political change achieved through court decisions in desegregation cases. A dynamic pairing, nonviolent protest and court action had a symbiotic relationship that was necessary for both to thrive and facilitate a successful end to the movement.

Often accompanied by local counsel, Motley was the LDF attorney who argued and won some of the most important desegregation cases. The winning of those cases was an integral part of the movement that produced a sea of change in both the law and public perception. In fact, much of the work to desegregate public schools, colleges, universities, housing, transportation, lunch counters, museums, libraries, parks, and other public accommodations was performed by Motley. It stands to reason that she would be famous for orchestrating that. However, that is simply not the case.

Despite her accomplishments, when the name Constance Baker Motley is mentioned, the response is often "Who was she?" or "What did she do?" Motley was a black woman, the daughter of immigrants from Nevis, British West Indies, a wife and a mother who became a pioneer and trailblazer in the legal profession. She broke down barriers, overcame sex discrimination, and operated outside the feminine role assigned to women by society and the civil rights movement. Her agency and action as a key strategist and trial lawyer affected the outcome of the movement. It facilitated the dismantling of Jim Crow and a segregated society.

Motley tried and won cases to end legalized segregation and vestiges of racial discrimination in the United States when neither the federal government nor state governments would do so. She used trial courts (and the appeal process) to integrate society and create integrated black and white public institutions and accommodations. She fought for dignity and equality under the law for all people. She was the trial or appellate counsel in fifty-seven cases in the US Supreme Court, eighty-two cases in federal courts of appeals, forty-eight cases in federal district courts, and numerous cases in state courts.[5]

Motley argued ten major civil rights cases before the US Supreme Court and won nine of them, an impeccable record.[6] In *Hamilton v. State of Alabama*, she protected the right of criminal defendants to have counsel in capital cases. She represented protesters who sat in at white-only restaurants and lunch counters. For instance, in *Turner v. City of Memphis*, the Supreme Court invalidated a regulation requiring racially segregated eating facilities and bathrooms in publicly operated facilities. In *Gober v. City of Birmingham, Shuttlesworth v. City of Birmingham, Bouie v. City of Columbia*, and *Barr v. City of Columbia*, other sit-in cases, she successfully challenged ordinances that required segregated seating in public eating places. Motley's victory in *Lupper v. Arkansas* was momentous. It led to the reversal of *all* the convictions that resulted from the sit-ins. In *Watson v. City of Memphis*, she obtained a ruling that required the immediate desegregation of municipal parks and recreational facilities. Her victory in *Calhoun v. Latimer* was significant in the desegregation of public schools in Atlanta. *Swain v. Alabama* was Motley's only loss in the US Supreme Court, and that was temporary. In that case she challenged an Alabama prosecutor's use of his peremptory challenges to remove all black candidates for jury duty. The court's decision upholding the prosecutor's use of peremptory challenges was reversed when the justices adopted her argument twenty years later in *Batson v. Kentucky*.[7] That reversal gave her a flawless record in the highest court in the land.

For almost twenty years Motley left behind the comfort of her home and family in the North and traveled throughout the dangerous South to fight Jim Crow. She represented the freedom riders who were arrested and jailed when they rode across the country on buses to test the Supreme Court decision that prohibited segregation in interstate transportation. She protected the right of protesters to march, boycott, and demonstrate in other ways. She represented civil rights activists and forced their release when they were arrested and locked up in Southern jails. Motley secured the right for blacks to register to vote, to have free and fair access to the polling stations, and to have access to the political power structure in general. She protected the right of blacks to freely occupy vacant seats on buses and trains, to use bathroom facilities and drink from water fountains in bus terminals and train stations, to be served and eat at lunch counters and restaurants, to stay in hotels, and to go to parks, museums, and all places of public accommodations on an equal basis with whites.[8]

Motley won cases against the states of Mississippi, Florida, Alabama, Louisiana, Arkansas, Georgia, Tennessee, North Carolina, South Carolina, Ohio, New Jersey, and New York as well as the District of Columbia and secured the right for blacks to attend formerly all-white public schools, colleges, and universities, including the Universities of Mississippi, Alabama, Georgia, and Florida and Clemson College. She once argued four appeals in one day, a herculean task that speaks to her stamina and her resolve to be the agent of change in the South. Between May 20 and 27, 1963, she won the decision to integrate Memphis parks, got a court order to admit black students to the University of Alabama, and represented Dr. Martin Luther King Jr. and maintained support for him in the Birmingham campaign and for the civil rights movement when she secured a federal appellate ruling reinstating 1,081 Birmingham schoolchildren who had been expelled for demonstrating and marching with him.[9] Motley also "forced the integration of public schools in New Rochelle," Hempstead, and Amityville, New York, and of public schools in Englewood, New Jersey, and central Virginia.[10]

Like other black women who made important contributions to the civil rights movement, Motley had to confront racism, sexism, and other obstacles in her work in the South. On many occasions, for instance, to accomplish a task as simple as making a telephone call while she was conducting a trial, she had to find and use a pay telephone. The courthouse was usually located in the center of the Jim Crow zone. Black attorneys did not have offices near the courthouse, and white lawyers did not permit her to use a telephone in their offices. As a result, Motley often had to walk for many blocks before she crossed an invisible line that divided the black and white communities in order to find a telephone that she could use to call the court of appeals and arrange to appeal an adverse ruling. She had to do this in the case to desegregate the University of Georgia as well as in the Birmingham school case.[11] This inconvenience was a constant reminder of the importance of her work in eliminating such insults toward blacks.

Motley had to endure the antics of hostile segregationist judges and lawyers in her work. She was disrespected by judges who turned their backs, faced the wall, and would not look at her when she argued her cases in front of them. She faced the prospect of violence and often "stayed in homes that had been bombed or were easy targets for attacks. . . . Her host in Mississippi, the civil rights activist Medgar Evers, was murdered by a sniper" shortly after she stayed in his home.[12] She frequently endured physical threats and encountered hostile mobs, hostile governors, and hostile school board officials. In Mississippi and Alabama, black men with guns surrounded the house she slept in to protect her.

Motley won long and hard-fought battles that led to the implementation of *Brown* and desegregation in the United States; however, Motley was marginalized in narratives about these battles and the civil rights movement. Much of the work that she and other black women performed in the civil rights movement was not fully documented. They did not receive proper recognition and credit from historians for their contributions to the movement's success. Historical narratives of the catalytic events that Motley and other women participated in do not fully examine the women's actions and agency.

Scholars who wrote the traditional male-centered narratives did not thoroughly examine Motley's life and experiences or include her in their accounts. Yet an abundance of scholarly literature has been written about well-known male lawyers involved in the civil rights movement. Their lives and experiences have been thoroughly examined. They have been credited for most of the legal victories secured and have been recorded as change agents and leaders in the traditional literature about the role of lawyers in the movement.

When historians wrote about the significant desegregation cases that Motley won, they focused primarily on her clients, many of whom became celebrated heroes (*e.g.*, James Meredith and Martin Luther King Jr.). Her name was not properly linked to her victories in the legal challenge to segregation. She was not properly connected with all the campaigns in which she performed crucial legal services or with the clients she represented. She, like other black women in the struggle for equality, was relegated to the background while the well-known men in the narratives were placed in the spotlight.

For example, historians wrote about how brave James Meredith was for integrating the University of Mississippi, but they did not examine Motley's work and experiences in the courts and the constant trips—nearly two dozen—that she made to Mississippi to get him into the university. Meredith rightfully deserves credit for his bravery; however, the narrative is incomplete without an examination of the behind-the-scenes work that Motley performed and her bravery in the face of the emotional stress, social tension, and physical danger she had to overcome in order to win the case and then to actually get him enrolled as a student. Historians wrote about the desegregation of public schools and the desegregation of the University of Alabama, the University of Georgia, and other institutions that were forced to admit blacks after Motley won cases against them, but they failed to explore her role and experience in securing the victories. In addition, historians wrote extensively about the impact of marches and other forms of protest led by King and the direct action of students who participated in sit-ins and freedom rides, but these historians did not fully explore the work that Motley performed or examine how her actions facilitated the protests to such a degree that they would not have succeeded without her intervention. She went to court and made it possible for the protesters to go forward with their activities and be released from jail when they were arrested or incarcerated.

Many of the people Motley helped had no idea who she was or what she did for them. She operated within the confines of courtrooms where many protesters were either banned or strongly discouraged from attending their trials. She was their unseen and unknown guardian angel.

Motley's beneficiaries include thousands of black graduates from formerly all-white public schools, colleges, universities, and professional schools that were forced to desegregate and admit blacks after she won cases against these institutions. Among them is Dr. Bernard Lafayette Jr., currently the national chairman of the Southern Christian Leadership Conference (SCLC) and a distinguished scholar in residence at Emory University in Atlanta. During the civil rights movement Lafayette served as the national coordinator of the SCLC, the national coordinator of the Poor People's Campaign, the director and organizer of the Alabama Voters Registration Project in Selma, Alabama, and the field secretary for the Student Nonviolent Coordinating Committee (SNCC) in Jackson, Mississippi. Others who benefited from Motley's dedication are thousands of activists who were arrested and jailed for participating in freedom rides, sit-ins, marches with King, and other forms of protest. Many of them know that the LDF represented them, but they do not know that it was Motley who actually argued and won the cases that secured their release from jail, overturned their convictions, facilitated the desegregation of formerly all-white institutions, promoted equality under the law for blacks, and advanced the goals of the civil rights movement, dismantling Jim Crow.

The narrative of the civil rights movement is fundamentally and irrevocably altered by the inclusion of Constance Baker Motley. Her story is like a breath of fresh air that only strengthens the legacy of the movement as a whole. Her contribution expands the view of history from the model of leadership by charismatic men to a more complete model that is inclusive of female change agents and leaders.

2

Black Women

On the Front Lines
but Not Properly Credited

> The civil rights movement of the fifties and sixties is merely the continuation of a long-standing tradition. Still, few published accounts of the civil rights era document the major role women played in the modern movement for social change.
> —Vicki L. Crawford, Jacqueline Anne Rouse, and Barbara Woods, *Women in the Civil Rights Movement: Trailblazers and Torchbearers, 1941–1965*

To comprehend the anatomy of the marginalization of Constance Baker Motley in the historical narratives of the civil rights movement, one must first understand the larger history of the movement and the lack of credit given to many black women who led struggles to abolish slavery, enact antilynching laws, abolish poll taxes and white primaries, and gain women's suffrage, fair housing, and temperance. Long before the civil rights movement of the 1950s–1960s, Sojourner Truth, Harriet Tubman, Anna Julia Haywood Cooper, Ida B. Wells-Barnett, Mary Church Terrell, Mary McLeod Bethune, and Dorothy I. Height were some of the black women who worked to eliminate racial discrimination and other social inequalities. They served as role models both for black female actors who fought to eliminate Jim Crow during the civil rights movement and for contemporary black female actors.

Historians conceived of the civil rights struggle as primarily a coalition of national organizations in a political movement that helped secure judicial and legislative victories. They focused on the NAACP and the LDF, the SCLC, SNCC, and other male-dominated national organizations.

Valeria Harvell has commented on the attention focused on the NAACP and the other organizations. She wrote that the NAACP is often cited as an early mobilizing entity that provided essential resources to local campaigns and much-needed leadership on the national and state levels. It provided a "mass-based membership, a communications infrastructure, and an organizational network with considerable fundraising capabilities."[1] The resources allowed the male-dominated NAACP to play an essential role in the movement; they also allowed its formal leaders to receive widespread media coverage and be perceived as its leaders.

In traditional narratives, historians primarily examined events of national significance and large demonstrations led by charismatic black ministers and other men who held formal titles in civil rights organizations. Those activities drew the attention of the largely white male-dominated mainstream media. They ignored or marginalized the lower-profile but indispensable activities engaged in primarily by black women. Those activities included recruiting participants to support the movement, establishing organizational procedures and routines, devising political strategies, raising funds, building alliances, mobilizing constituencies to sustain the movement, educating and preparing blacks to become voters, and participating in direct action protests.[2]

Historians generally agree that certain events were catalysts for the civil rights movement. These include the 1954 *Brown v. Board of Education* Supreme Court ruling, the 1955 Montgomery Bus Boycott, the 1957 crisis surrounding the integration of Central High School in Little Rock, Arkansas, the lunch-counter sit-ins initiated by college students, the freedom rides, the crisis surrounding the desegregation of the University of Alabama, the crisis surrounding the desegregation of the University of Georgia, and the crisis surrounding the desegregation of the University of Mississippi. Motley played a critical role as an LDF lawyer in each of these catalytic events and most, if not all, of the other significant events that occurred during the movement. Other black women also risked their lives and played crucial roles in these and other catalytic events in the struggle for racial equality.

Black women participated in significant school desegregation lawsuits that Motley won. They also participated in various forms of direct action such as boycotts, marches, sit-ins, and freedom rides to force change and end de jure segregation. They were fired from their jobs, teargassed, assaulted with water from high-power fire department hoses, attacked by vicious police dogs, raped, beaten, arrested, convicted, and jailed for protesting segregation and for attempting to register to vote, eat at white-only lunch counters, drink from white-only water fountains, ride in white-only sections of public buses and trains, and use white-only public facilities.

The women were "agents of change; they fought valiantly on all fronts," wrote Aprele Elliott.[3] They acted because they wanted to transform American society. They wanted to eliminate segregation, end racial oppression, obtain equal rights and justice, and change the way blacks were discriminated against and forced to live their daily lives.

Among the black women whose agency and actions were important were mothers who objected to their children walking across dangerous railroad tracks or riding buses past all-white schools with superior academic programs, buildings, and supplies to get to racially segregated, dilapidated, and poorly equipped all-black schools. The women took the initiative, challenged racial discrimination and disparity in public education in their local communities, and became plaintiffs in *Brown*. They accelerated change in the circumstances under which their children and other black public school children were educated.

Black women who were emotionally, spiritually, and physically tired of the policy that forced blacks to stand and give their seats on public buses to whites joined forces with Jo Ann Gibson Robinson, set a goal to end the policy, and designed and implemented the plan to achieve the goal. They assumed responsibility to carry out the plan, organized and led the Montgomery Bus Boycott after the arrest of Rosa Parks, and forced the abandonment of the objectionable policy.

Six young black women were among the nine students who voluntarily joined the protest that Daisy Bates orchestrated to desegregate Central High School in Little Rock. As a result of the brave action of the young women and Bates, the formerly all-white school was forced to admit black students and provide them the same quality of education available to white students.

Black college women who wanted to end the discriminatory policy that prevented black shoppers in stores from enjoying a meal at public lunch counters participated in sit-ins that Diane Nash organized and led at all-white lunch counters to protest and change the policy. Their action resulted in a Supreme Court ruling and a civil rights act that required the lunch counters and restaurants to serve blacks in the same manner in which they served whites.

Black women who opposed state laws and practices that prohibited blacks from riding in the front of interstate buses or from sitting in the all-white section of bus terminals or using the all-white restroom facilities participated in freedom rides organized and led by Ruby Doris Smith Robinson and Nash. Their action in challenging the laws forced Congress to adopt legislation to prohibit racial discrimination in interstate transportation and facilities and forced bus companies across the country to openly accommodate black passengers in the same way they accommodated whites.

Autherine Lucy and Charlayne Hunter were among the black women who wanted to attend all-white colleges and universities and who filed lawsuits against state educational institutions that refused to accept black students. As a result of their actions challenging discriminatory admission policies, blacks were admitted to formerly all-white colleges, universities, and professional schools.

Ella Baker, Septima Clark, and other black women who wanted to change the policies and practices that prevented blacks from voting organized voter education programs and drives to help blacks register and vote. As a result of their actions, political power was developed in black communities. Black candidates were elected to local, state, and national positions, where they advocated for services and programs to benefit black communities.

Feminist scholars have discussed the myriad ways in which black female activists were leaders and change agents in the ongoing struggle for racial equality and the manner in which their contributions to the civil rights movement have been omitted. Vicki Crawford, Jacqueline Anne Rouse, and Barbara Woods, quoted at the beginning of this chapter, wrote, "They have organized and led struggles for suffrage, fair housing, temperance, antilynching laws, as well as to abolish poll taxes, white primaries, Jim Crow laws, and to obtain full employment for themselves and their men, and for equal educational facilities for their children."[4] Francoise Hamlin did similar work and concluded that black women received little coverage or recognition for their accomplishments because of their sex.[5] Aprele Elliott argued that black women received little coverage or credit for their accomplishments in historical accounts of the movement because of sexism within and outside the movement and because of the traditional charismatic perspective of leadership. She examined the experiences of Ella Baker, who was revered by many civil rights activists but was largely ignored by historians because of the constraints imposed on women that rendered them "invisible to all but regional audiences and movement insiders."[6] Bernice McNair Barnett asserted that in scholarship about the civil rights movement, the experiences and leadership roles of black women had virtually been "neglected, forgotten, or considered inconsequential or of secondary importance relative to those of men."[7] She argued that women remained anonymous and invisible (while high-profile men were visible) in part because of gender and racial biases in social movement literature and scholarship that continued to concentrate on the roles played by elite and charismatic black men.

Recent literature produced by these and other scholars substantiates the assertion that black women initiated and sustained some of the most significant events of the civil rights movement but were marginalized or completely overlooked in narratives about those events.[8] Some authors asserted that much of the work the women performed was not accurately documented because they were women. Barnett, in particular, argued that black women's work was not documented because despite the fact that they performed dangerous organizing and mobilizing work in the early stages of activities in many local campaigns, they were forced into the background when nationally recognized men with formal titles arrived, took over, and made public speeches.[9]

The scholars criticize the civil rights community and historians for failure to credit black women for the important work they performed. They are especially critical of narratives that do not explore the experiences of Daisy Bates or examine the contributions and experiences of activists such as Ella Baker, Diane Nash,

Jo Ann Robinson, and Ruby Doris Robinson. The name Constance Baker Motley can be added to the list.

Bernard Lafayette Jr., a civil rights leader, acknowledged that female activists whom he knew and worked with were marginalized in historical accounts of the movement. He stated that Baker, Nash, and Robinson in particular were not recognized or respected for the contributions they made. "Ella Baker, the executive director of the Southern Christian Leadership Council, organized the Student Nonviolent Coordinating Committee, and she organized more NAACP chapters in the South than anyone else, but she did not get the recognition she deserved for her work," he said.[10]

When he was a college student, Lafayette participated in the Nashville student sit-in movement led by Diane Nash. He was part of the second group of freedom riders she organized after the first group was viciously beaten by a mob and its bus was firebombed and destroyed.[11] Lafayette was also a founding member of SNCC and a participant in many SNCC activities that Ruby Doris Robinson organized.

"Diane, Ruby Doris, and other courageous black women were constantly in danger because of their leadership work; they were harassed, beaten, and sentenced to hard labor in some of the worst prisons in the South because of their activities. They did not receive proper recognition for all that they did and endured," he recalled.[12] He acknowledged that when a narrative did include black female actors, their participation was often primarily discussed from the point of view of men writing about well-known men.

These male-centered narratives portrayed women as contributors to the work performed by men. Sometimes black men even received extensive media coverage and became widely known for leading activities that black women had actually led and sustained.[13] Examples are the historical narratives about the Montgomery Bus Boycott and the accounts of protest marches, student sit-ins, freedom rides, and voter registration drives. The roles of well-known men with formal titles were emphasized in the narratives, and many of the black women who initiated, organized, and participated in the events were viewed as secondary actors or completely ignored.

Traditional narratives of the movement also failed to explore the manner in which experiences and opportunities were different for black women and men because of the patriarchal constraints of gender, race, and class and the theology, doctrine, and traditions of black churches.[14] These constraints disproportionately and negatively affected women in the context of power; they determined and restricted the resources, experiences, leadership opportunities, and visibility that women had in the movement. Conversely, the constraints affected men positively in the context of power. Formal titles and leadership positions were reserved for and available only to men, especially in black churches and on the national level in civil rights organizations, where men had power and resources and enjoyed high visibility in the civil rights community and the media.

Gender constraints were a particularly important factor in the differences for men and women in terms of access to structural and institutional power and visibility, in part because of the important role these constraints played in the structure of black churches and civil rights organizations. They were a determining and limiting factor in the opportunities open to women in the organizations and institutions and in the perception of women and their contributions to the movement. Belinda Robnett argued that gender was a "defining construct of power relations" that "shaped the structure of the movement."[15] It was an exclusionary construct of power relations that channeled women away from formal leadership in organizations and confined them to informal leadership because they were women.

Black churches were absolutely essential institutions in the civil rights movement. In addition to providing spaces for spiritual and social gatherings on Sundays, churches were the sites of mass meetings and strategy sessions for campaigns.

Ministers, especially pastors of black churches, were charismatic leaders of their congregations; they inspired people to follow them. They were regarded as leaders in the black communities in the South in which black church members were the majority and were accustomed to regarding ministers as leaders.[16]

Black ministers had access to resources: money, the pulpits they regularly spoke in, and the church facilities where mass meetings were held and covered by the press. They were able to mobilize large groups for political action. They regularly represented and spoke on behalf of the community, and they had more influence and power than any other members of the black community.[17]

Black women were not permitted to be ministers in most black churches; doctrines and traditions in the churches dictated that only men could be members of the clergy.[18] Societal norms also made it acceptable for women to be subordinated, confined to the background, and oppressed by men in the male-dominated hierarchy of black churches. These norms perpetuated the expectation that only men would occupy formal leadership positions: ministers, deacons, trustees, and top decision makers. They reinforced the patriarchal belief that a woman's place was in the pews or the kitchen of the church and in her home as mother, housewife, supporter, and inspiration for her husband, who was deemed to be the head of the household and the leader women should follow.[19] Thus, both church doctrines and societal norms prevented women from attaining the power and status enjoyed by black ministers and from having access to the same resources as men.

The NAACP, SCLC, and other national civil rights organizations that received widespread media attention during the movement were also male-dominated; they often either drew from the leadership pool of black churches or modeled their leadership qualifications on those of the churches. The result was that the relationship of women and men in those organizations was the same as it was in black churches: Black men were the formal leaders, with traditional titles, power, and authority on the national level. Black women were constrained in the roles they could assume on the national level because of their sex. They participated largely in roles behind the scenes. When they were given responsibility in organizations, they were generally assigned clerical duties or relegated to serve on committees that handled such matters as education, membership, welfare, fund-raising, and organizational-type work—traditional "women's work."[20] The work roles assigned to them were considered to be supportive of or contributing to the formal leadership provided by men, thus reinforcing societal gender norms and expectations.[21]

The NAACP, in particular, was a bureaucratic organization that seemingly embraced male chauvinism. Executive officers on the national level were all men. Although women were excluded from formal leadership titles on the national level, educated, middle-class, self-employed, and even poor uneducated black women held important leadership positions on the local and regional levels in communities around the country. Many of the women were elected as secretaries of local NAACP branches. They were an indispensable asset for the local recruitment of members and fundraising drives that were the lifeblood of the NAACP, keeping it alive and functioning during the movement.[22] The gender constraints prevented women from holding formal titles on the national level, yet the NAACP recognized the importance of women on the grassroots level. It therefore encouraged organizers and fieldworkers to exploit the resources that black women offered as grassroots leaders.[23]

Some black women counteracted the oppression in society and the sex discrimination in the movement by adopting various types of nontraditional leadership styles that were different from the conventional models employed by men. The styles they utilized included organizing membership drives, teaching in freedom schools, and directing voter registration campaigns. Some participated in boycotts, marches, sit-ins, and other types of direct action leadership. Others mobilized the masses in small towns and cities to participate in and support the movement.

Andrew Young, the executive director of the SCLC during the civil rights movement and later an ambassador to the United Nations and the mayor of Atlanta, noted, "It was the women going door to door, speaking with their neighbors, meeting in voter-registration classes, and organizing through their churches, that gave the vital momentum and energy to the movement, and that made it a mass movement."[24] Without women's work, there might not have been enough participants for a mass movement.

Black women also utilized a style of leadership known as *bridge leadership*.

As bridge leaders, they connected social movement organizations and their potential constituents: communities of black people needed to support the movement and bring about change.[25]

Many blacks, especially those in Southern rural areas, were not predisposed to join the civil rights movement because they feared for their lives, their jobs, or both. They were afraid that the outsiders who came to their communities would stir up trouble and get them killed. Male-dominated national organizations and their leaders often could not mobilize the masses or gain the support of blacks in the rural South because they were the outsiders who had no connections to people in the local communities; they did not understand the issues that affected people in the local communities, and they were not trusted by them.[26]

Grassroots leaders, primarily black female organizers and bridge leaders who had little or no direct access to the power politics of formal organizations on the national level, were the insiders who had the confidence and loyalty of the masses in many local and rural communities. They went into local areas and provided the necessary strategies to connect people in isolated rural areas to movement organizations; they recruited and mobilized participants to make it a mass movement.[27]

Although gender constraints put obstacles in their way, some resourceful black women overcame them and became traditional leaders, held formal titles in organizations on the local level, and led innovative and successful programs that transformed American society. They included the following: Daisy Bates, the president of the local NAACP branch and a leader of the black community in Little Rock during the crisis to desegregate Central High School; Fanny Lou Hamer, the vice chairwoman of the Mississippi Freedom Democratic Party, a recognized leader on the local level in Mississippi, and a spokeswoman for the party at the Democratic National Convention; Diane Nash, the chairwoman of the Central Committee of the Nashville Student Movement and a leader of sits-ins and freedom rides; Ruby Doris Robinson, the leader of the Spelman Student Movement who also helped Nash develop field operations for strategies employed in the sit-ins and freedom rides they organized; and Jo Ann Robinson, the president of the Women's Political Council and a leader of the Montgomery Bus Boycott.

Feminist scholars wrote these and other black women into their narratives of the civil rights movement. Their accounts offered new and different ways of understanding leadership and "how attention to gender advances [that] understanding."[28] They challenged male-centered narratives, the perception that there was a singular leadership style, and the belief that the movement was led only by men in national organizations. Their findings demonstrate that a large contingent of diverse black women participated in the civil rights movement as leaders, that there were many different levels and styles of leadership employed in the movement, and that black women's action and agency as leaders mattered.

The eclectic group of black women who led the movement included professionals, students, schoolteachers, college professors, businesswomen, church workers, domestic workers, service workers, clubwomen, entertainers, housewives, factory workers, sharecroppers, welfare recipients, Head Start activists, beauticians, and family members (grandmothers, mothers, daughters, and sisters).[29] Leadership styles exhibited by the women ranged from traditional formal leadership of organizations on the local and regional levels, charismatic influence, and power leadership to bridge leadership, grassroots leadership, behind-the-scenes leadership, and participation as foot soldiers. They risked their lives, economic security, families, and homes and performed important work that helped transform the United States into a more equal and just society.

Some uncelebrated and unrecognized black female actors worked in nontraditional political areas for women during the civil rights movement. Constance Baker Motley was one of them; she worked as a legal strategist and a litigator in courtrooms across the nation at a time when the legal profession was almost exclusively the province of white men. There were very few black lawyers, there were very few female lawyers, and there were almost no female litigators (lawyers who argue cases in court) when she began her work at the LDF in the 1940s.

For most of her career, Motley was the only female lawyer at the LDF and the only female trial lawyer in the courts. In a 1991 article for *Ms.* magazine, she commented, "In the 1940s women lawyers were a joke in most courthouses and unheard of in virtually every place except New York City." When she tried a case in Jackson, Mississippi, in 1948, it was such a novelty that "the whole town turned out to see the Negro lawyers from New York, one of whom was a woman."[30]

3
Early Life and Preparation to Become a Leader

I am supposed to tell you about some of my personal experiences over the last forty years as a black woman and a woman in the legal profession but let me note that during that period I have spent most of my time trying to decide who is in the good guy camp and who is in the bad guy camp. As a result, my view of the world is that men fall into two camps, the good guys and the bad guys.

Now one thing that most people have been curious about regarding my career and have always asked me about is how I happened to study law. . . . Let me say that my becoming a lawyer was the result of commitment of one of the good guys [a white man named Clarence Blakeslee].

—Constance Baker Motley, quoted in J. Clay Smith Jr., *Rebels in Law: Voices in History of Black Women Lawyers*

Just before I graduated from Columbia Law School, I was fortunate enough to get a job as a law clerk on the staff of the NAACP Legal Defense and Educational Fund. The chief counsel was Thurgood Marshall. And there was another one of those good guys, because if it had not been for Thurgood Marshall's liberal view of how women ought to have the same chance as men to become lawyers, I probably would not be standing here today telling you about my career.

—Constance Baker Motley, quoted in Smith, *Rebels in Law*

Born in New Haven, Connecticut, on September 14, 1921, Constance Baker was the ninth of twelve children of Rachel Keziah Huggins Baker and Willoughby Alva Baker, both of whom were immigrants from Nevis, British West Indies.[1] In a story familiar to many immigrants, her father emigrated first, arriving in New Haven in 1906. Her mother arrived a year later in 1907 to marry her father.[2]

There were few job opportunities for blacks when the Baker family settled in New Haven. "Prior to World War II there was nothing for blacks to do except domestic work or work at Yale," Constance recalled. Her father got a job at Yale, where he became the chef of Skull and Bones, the school's elite secret society; he remained at that job throughout his work life.[3]

While growing up in New Haven, Constance was keenly aware that the only jobs available to her father and other blacks were service jobs or domestic work, even if they were educated and qualified for positions that were exclusively reserved for whites. Her awareness of the limited opportunities available to blacks because of their race motivated her to want to become a lawyer and fight to change the system of racial discrimination in employment.

Constance's parents were Episcopalians. They were brought up in the Anglican Church, the main Christian denomination on the British-ruled island of Nevis. When they arrived in New Haven, they joined St. Luke's Episcopal Church, the only black Episcopal Church in the city. St. Luke's was not only the church that the Baker family attended when she was a child, it was also the church where she married Joel Wilson Motley Jr. in 1946 and where her funeral was held on October 5, 2005.[4]

All the West Indians that she and her family knew belonged to St. Luke's. It was where West Indians from Nevis, Jamaica, Grenada, Montserrat, and other islands gathered and socialized on Sundays.[5] They had what Constance referred to as a common background.

Life in the Baker home was what Constance described as traditional in West Indian families. Her mother, Rachel, was a homemaker and the caretaker of the children; she was always home. She had originally planned to become a schoolteacher, but she relinquished that goal when she married Willoughby, moving to the United States to be with him.[6] Willoughby was a very strong father figure, the head of the household. He earned the money and decided how it was going to be spent. He allocated a fixed amount of money for his wife each day. If she needed an additional amount of money to buy shoes or other items for the family, she had to sit down with Willoughby and explain what the money was to be used for.[7]

Public schools in New Haven were integrated. Constance attended schools in the late 1920s and the 1930s in an "overwhelmingly white community" near her home.[8] It was an ethnically diverse community composed of Irish, Jewish, Polish, and West Indian families.

Education was very important in the Baker home because her parents realized that it was an important tool for advancement. Both of them had finished the English standard school in Nevis, which is comparable to completion of the eighth or ninth grade in the United States. Willoughby, in particular, understood the value of education, so he willingly used his limited financial resources for his children's education. All of Constance's brothers and sisters, except for her youngest sister, who had health issues, were well educated and had successful careers.[9]

Rachel and Willoughby settled in the part of New Haven where immigrants settled. Constance said that it became a tradition for her family and other West Indians in New Haven to go to the Welcome Hall on Sunday afternoon at 3:00 P.M. The Welcome Hall provided different types of educational programs for West Indian children, and it also provided a camp for them in the summer.[10]

One Sunday after leaving the Welcome Hall, Constance had her first experience with discrimination when she went to a public beach (in either Branford or Milford, Connecticut) with some white youth in a racially mixed group. The white youth were permitted to enter the beach. Constance, however, was not; she was turned away because she was black.[11] This exclusion from the beach was a motivating factor in her decision to become a civil rights lawyer: she wanted to attack the system of racial injustice that permitted whites to enter public spaces but prevented blacks from entering them solely because of their race.

Before the beach experience, Constance had not been exposed to any white-only or "colored-only" facilities or places. She had not personally been subjected to any racial segregation that she recognized. She was not knowledgeable about the black experience in the United States and the kind of racial discrimination that black people lived with on a daily basis, especially in the South, because she had not been taught black history in school or at home. She was first exposed to black history at St. Luke's when a new minister came from St. Augustine College in North Carolina. Constance was a teenager at the time. Shortly after arriving, the minister realized that black history was not being taught in New Haven schools, so he instituted a program at the church. Every Friday night at the young people's fellowship meeting, he taught black history to Constance and the other youth.[12]

One of the teachers at the Welcome Hall was Alice White. On Saturday afternoons she invited the children to her house and read literature to them. During the visits, Miss White talked to them about President Abraham Lincoln and his belief that law was one of the most difficult professions. Later in life Constance reflected on the influence Miss White had on her life. She believed that by reading to her and talking to her about Lincoln, Miss White had inspired her to become a lawyer. She credited Miss White with having more influence directly on her life than any of her regular schoolteachers.[13]

While growing up in New Haven, Constance was aware of only two black lawyers in the city; both were men. One of them, George W. Crawford, a graduate of Yale Law School, was very prominent and successful.

After being introduced to black history by her minister at church and being influenced by Miss White, Constance decided that she too wanted to become a lawyer and join the fight for equality and justice for blacks. She made that decision at age fifteen.[14] When she informed her teachers of the decision, they didn't think much of it because they could not envision a black woman being a lawyer. Her family did not encourage her to pursue a career in law, either. In fact, her mother thought she should become a hairdresser. No one seemed to think it was a good idea for Constance, a young black woman, to aspire to become a lawyer, so she received no encouragement.[15]

The lack of encouragement did not deter Constance, however. In fact, the effect was just the opposite. "I was the kind of person who would not be put down," she stated. "I rejected the notion that my race or my sex would bar my success in life."[16]

In September 1936, when she enrolled at Hillhouse High School in New Haven, Constance held fast to her resolve to become a lawyer. She pursued an interest in political affairs, race relations, black history, and the legal profession. She read books about black history in the United States, especially those written by W. E. B. Du Bois and James Weldon Johnson, and she began to debate adults on current events.[17] She also took on Du Bois's challenge to become one of what he called the *talented tenth*.

Du Bois, a Harvard-educated scholar and political activist, had challenged Booker T. Washington's philosophy that blacks should limit themselves to trade and agricultural schools and careers to achieve economic parity with whites and that they should adjust their attitudes in order to accommodate, appease, and get along with whites. The sometimes bitter rivalry of Du Bois and Washington played out in the public sphere.

Washington articulated his position in his 1895 Atlanta Compromise Speech, in which he argued, "In all things purely social, we [blacks and whites] can be as separate as the five fingers, and yet one as the hand in all things essential to mutual progress."[18] Many in the South interpreted Washington's philosophy as a complete surrender of blacks' demand for civil and political equality with whites, and therefore an endorsement of segregation and a limitation of the aspirations of blacks.

Du Bois asserted that blacks should not only seek economic parity with whites but also demand full and complete social and political equality. He argued that one-tenth of black men—the talented tenth—should receive university educations, become professionals (lawyers, doctors, and teachers), gain positions of full authority with whites, and fulfill their duty to help less fortunate and uneducated blacks improve their lives and the conditions under which they lived. Du Bois believed that all blacks would benefit because the talented tenth would become leaders in the fight for equal rights for the black race. To assist in achieving this goal, he and his supporters met in Niagara Falls, New York, in 1905 and formed an organization to oppose racial segregation and the accommodation and compromise with whites policy advocated by Washington. The Niagara Movement, as it was called, was the first black civil rights organization of the twentieth century. It was the precursor of the NAACP, which Du Bois also helped found.[19]

In addition to black history and Du Bois, the Supreme Court case, *Missouri ex rel. Gaines v. Canada* reinforced Constance's determination to become a civil rights lawyer and an advocate for social and political change. In this case Lloyd Gaines, the plaintiff, had been refused admission to the University of Missouri Law School because he was black. The state of Missouri offered to pay his tuition at another law school, but Gaines rejected that offer.[20] The ruling in *Gaines* was rendered during Constance's junior year in high school.

The Supreme Court struck down the policy that permitted the state to pay for blacks to attend out-of-state graduate schools rather than admitting them to Missouri's in-state white-only schools. Gaines had argued that the policy of providing out-of-state scholarship funds for him, a black person, in lieu of admitting him to the state's white-only law school violated his Fourteenth Amendment rights. The Supreme Court agreed. It held that when a state provides in-state graduate education for whites, it must also provide in-state graduate education for blacks.

The *Gaines* decision drew support from blacks in the South and in the North. Constance recalled that black people in New Haven were very excited about the decision. They gathered at the Dixwell Community Center, where black people would meet whenever any community issue came up, to discuss it. The center had been built by Clarence Blakeslee, a successful white businessman and long-established philanthropist in New Haven. George Crawford, the city's prominent black lawyer, attended the meeting and explained the *Gaines* decision to the New Haven residents.[21]

To the dismay of Constance and others in attendance, Crawford said that the decision didn't have the meaning that they thought it had. The Supreme Court had not held that all-white state universities had to desegregate and admit black students. It had simply held that it was impermissible for the state of Missouri to send Gaines, a black student, out of the state to attend law school if there was an in-state law school for whites. The decision merely required that an educational institution be provided for Gaines to attend within Missouri; it did not outlaw segregated schools in Missouri.

The *Gaines* ruling reflected, and was consistent with, the Supreme Court's 1896 "separate but equal" ruling in *Plessy v. Ferguson*, which did not require states to desegregate all-white public facilities and admit blacks; it only required them to provide blacks with separate facilities.

Constance was disappointed that the *Gaines* decision upheld the *Plessy* doctrine. It was an additional incentive for her to become a lawyer, challenge racial discrimination in education, and work to change the system of racial exclusion that required blacks and whites to be separated in public facilities and institutions simply because of their race.

Shortly after the *Gaines* decision, Constance graduated from Hillhouse High School with honors and an intense determination to become a lawyer. Her plan was to attend college right away; however, in 1939, when she graduated, the nation was still steeped in the Great Depression, and her family could not afford to pay her tuition. She had written to several colleges inquiring about scholarships, but the financial assistance they could provide was not sufficient to cover her expenses. Although the lack of encouragement to become a lawyer was no obstacle for her resolve to achieve her career goal, poverty was. Without financial resources, she did not have the means to attend college.[22]

Instead of continuing her education, then, Constance looked for a job so she could earn money for tuition. The only job she was offered was with the National Youth Administration, where she would learn to refinish furniture; she accepted the job and earned $50 a month in that training program.[23] She also immersed herself in community and church activities, attended lots of meetings, became very active in civic affairs, and became president of the New Haven Youth Council. Constance participated in political activities when groups lobbied state legislators in Hartford, the state capital, and she became the secretary of the New Haven Community Council, a group formed by New Haven residents to deal with black unemployment, the lack of adequate housing, and other issues that affected the quality of life for blacks.[24]

Constance also became involved in national affairs during the period in which she could not afford to attend college. In that work, she experienced racial discrimination outside Connecticut that she recognized. It occurred at a lunch counter when she was president of the Negro Youth Council. She had traveled from Chicago to Washington, DC, in 1940 with a peace organization that was concerned about the US intervention in World War II, and she had accepted an invitation to have tea with First Lady Eleanor Roosevelt at the White House. On the way, Constance and the others in the group stopped in Indiana to eat at a restaurant. The white members of the group were permitted to sit at the counter and eat, but when Constance and the other black members attempted to sit down, the man behind the counter said, "We don't serve Negroes in here." One of the black members of the group called the police to complain about the refusal to serve them. A police officer came in response to his call and said, "They're not going to serve you here. If you want to stay and fight it, fine, but I would advise you to leave and go across the state line. . . . They have an ordinance in this town which says that Negroes are not to be found here after sundown."[25]

The denial of service at the lunch counter personalized the impact of American racial segregation for Constance. Before that incident, she had never been in a situation in which black people could not sit and eat with white people. She had grown up in New Haven, where blacks and whites sat and ate together in restaurants. She had never before been refused service because of her race. The lunch-counter incident further motivated her to become a civil rights lawyer and challenge racial discrimination in public accommodations.

The time between graduating from high school in 1939 and going to college in February 1941 was a particularly stressful period in Constance's life. She was desperate to continue her education, but the longer she stayed out of school, the more she was afraid her chances of going to college would diminish.[26]

"Her big break came when . . . she spoke at a meeting" and "so impressed builder and philanthropist Clarence W. Blakeslee that he offered to finance her college education and pay her law school tuition as well," the magazine of Columbia University reported.[27] The meeting she spoke at was held at the Dixwell Community Center that Blakeslee had built for blacks in New Haven.

The center was a beautiful building with a gymnasium and meeting rooms, but blacks in New Haven were not using the center. A perplexed Blakeslee wanted to know why, so he called a meeting to find out. The meeting was chaired by the lawyer George Crawford, who was on the board of directors of the center.[28] The rest of the board was made up predominantly of white people from Yale.

Blakeslee sat through the entire meeting and listened to people express their opinions about why the community center was not being used. Constance, the youngest person at the meeting, stood up and proclaimed that it wasn't being used because blacks didn't have a vested interest in the center. She pointed out that blacks from the community were not on the board of directors, so they "didn't have anything to say about the programs and . . . didn't feel that it was their institution" because they had "no role . . . in decision making at the community center." What was needed for blacks to use the center, said Constance, was for more blacks from the community to be on the board and to participate in the control of the center and its programs.[29]

Years later, in an interview about her comments at the meeting, Constance remarked, "It was not the thing to say to these good white people who had established this place," and "it was very embarrassing" to the black adults, who were annoyed with her for speaking up. They feared Blakeslee was offended by her comments.[30]

Blakeslee was not offended, however. Instead, the day after the meeting he sought Constance out and asked to meet with her. He was so impressed with her presentation that he invited her to his office and offered to pay for her education.[31] When asked later if she had been afraid to meet with Blakeslee after she had made potentially offensive comments at the meeting, Constance replied, "I wasn't afraid, because I guess that was my nature, not to be afraid." She described the meeting with Blakeslee: "And I went there, and he said, 'I was impressed with what you had to say.' He said to me, 'Well, you know, this morning I called the principal of the high school and I see you graduated from high school with honors. Why aren't you in college?' I said, 'I don't have the money. ' He said, 'Well, you know, I would be willing to pay for your college education for as long as you want to go.' Just like that out of the clear blue sky. And he said,

'What do you want to do?' I said, 'I want to be a lawyer.' And he said, 'Well, I'm sending my grandson to Harvard to law school and I guess I can send you if that's what you want to do.'"[32]

One of the things that Constance always remembered about the meeting with Blakeslee was his statement "You know, Abraham Lincoln said that an independent voice is God's gift to the nation. . . . I don't want you ever to forget that."[33] Throughout her entire career, Constance Baker Motley was an independent voice.

In 1993, as she was being inducted into the National Women's Hall of Fame, Constance used the occasion to publicly acknowledge the essential role that Blakeslee had played in her life. He was responsible for her success, she said, noting that he had "made millions of dollars, and what he did with those millions was to help educate black Americans."[34]

While she was in high school, Constance had applied to all-black colleges. That decision was influenced by the African American literature she had been introduced to by her minister at St. Luke's, which taught her about the impact of racial segregation in the United States. It was also influenced by the disappointing *Gaines* decision. She was motivated to go to a black college and learn more about the black experience in America.

Fisk University in Nashville was one of the black colleges Constance had applied to and been accepted by during her senior year in high school. With Blakeslee's financial assistance, she enrolled at Fisk in 1941. During the train ride to Nashville, she experienced Jim Crow segregation and the extent to which it affected the lives, activities, and freedom of movement of black people south of the Mason-Dixon Line when she was forced to either ride in the all-black car or get off the train.

Constance had boarded the train in New York and sat in an integrated car until the train pulled into the station in Cincinnati, where she was told to disembark so that another passenger car could be attached. The train crew put that passenger car, which was much older and rustier than the other cars on the train, right behind the engine. When Constance attempted to get back to her original seat in the integrated car, a black porter said to her, "You have to go in this car," pointing to the old rusty one that had just been added with COLORED written on the coach door.[35] Constance described that experience as follows:

> Well, when I went to Fisk, it was my first train South, and I took a train from New Haven to New York. . . . I don't remember whether I had to change in New York or not—but I do remember when I got to Cincinnati I had to go into the Jim Crow car because from Cincinnati that train was going south to Nashville, so I had to come out of the car in which I was riding and go into a car on which there was a sign that said "Colored."

And that was my first real experience with segregation in the United States. I had never before experienced [Southern-style, Jim Crow] segregation.

I was alone and I went into this car, and there were very few blacks in there. I remember there was an elderly man [who] . . . said to me, "Oh, yes, you come right in here, as if to say, "This is the way it is and we have to accept it. . . . Well, I did. . . . So here we were in Cincinnati, which was not the South, but you were required then to get in the Jim Crow car because the next stop, I guess, was going to be in Kentucky . . . and that was where the segregation was required.[36]

Although Constance knew that she would have to get into a Jim Crow car at some point on her train ride from New York to Tennessee, she was both frightened and humiliated when it actually happened. Those emotions escalated to indignation several years later when she was again subjected to riding in a Jim Crow car or being screened in to shield her from whites on a train. "I remember being infuriated from the top of my head to the tip of my toes the first time a screen was put around . . . me on a train leaving Washington in the 1940s," she said.[37]

On her first trip home from Nashville, Constance took her parents a souvenir of Southern life: a sign that read COLORED ONLY.[38] It was a visual and tangible representation of the dehumanizing nature of Jim Crow—being forced to get out of her seat in an integrated train car and move to a seat in the racially segregated car because she was black. That introduction to legal racism in the United States reinforced her determination to pursue law as a career and fight to eradicate racial segregation in transportation, public accommodations, and all aspects of society.

Once she arrived in Nashville, Constance discovered that being black prevented her from attending the theater, eating at all-white lunch counters and restaurants, trying on clothes or shoes in department stores, and doing all the things she had done routinely in New Haven. Dressing rooms in Southern department stores were only for white shoppers. Black customers had to give the clerk their size and buy clothing without having the opportunity to try it on—hoping it would fit when they got it home. After a couple of times shopping in Nashville, Constance resolved that she would not continue to subject herself to that humiliating treatment and that if she needed clothes, she would wait until she went back to New Haven to buy them.[39] She restricted herself almost exclusively to the Fisk campus until she grew too exasperated to continue her education in the South. She resented the predicament she found herself in because of racial discrimination in the South and decided to go back to the North and transfer to New York University (NYU).

In 1942 Constance left Fisk and enrolled at NYU.[40] The decision was influenced by multiple factors: the Jim Crow segregation she experienced in the South, the US intervention in World War II, and the departure of many of the best professors from Fisk to take positions elsewhere. Constance feared that Fisk would lose its accreditation and that she would not be able to compete for admission to Columbia Law School if she remained there.[41]

Her experience interacting with black students at Fisk proved to be beneficial years later when she was a lawyer with the LDF and had a large number of cases in the South where hotels were segregated by law. Jim Crow segregation prevented her from staying in hotels when she went South to represent clients in court, so she had to find private homes to stay in. Fiskites lived in many of the communities, and they opened their homes to her and other LDF lawyers and NAACP staff members.[42]

While enrolled at NYU, Constance lived uptown in Harlem at the Young Women's Christian Association (YWCA) on 137th Street. It was there that she met her future husband, Joel Motley Jr., who lived uptown at the Young Men's Christian Association (YMCA).[43]

In October 1943 Constance graduated from NYU with honors and a bachelor of arts degree in economics.[44] She could not go directly to law school at Columbia because the fall semester had already begun; she had to wait until February 1944 to enroll.

While waiting to start law school, Constance took a job with the Office of Dependency Benefits (ODB) in Newark, New Jersey, a new wartime agency to aid servicemen's dependents. After she took the mandatory placement test for the position, her supervisor, "a white woman from the Bronx[,] came up to her all excited" and exclaimed, "You are going to get a promotion." Constance asked why and was told, "Because you got a ninety-five on the exam." Then the supervisor added, "The only thing is that the promotion won't come through until February." Constance replied, "Well, I'm not going to be here in February. I'm going to Columbia Law School in February."[45] Similar to the reaction of her school-teachers years earlier when Constance had proclaimed her decision to become a lawyer, the supervisor scoffed, "That's the dumbest thing I ever heard, a complete waste of time.... Women don't get anywhere in the law."[46] She continued, "That's crazy. Why do you want to waste your time doing that? You should stay here. Women like you are moving right up here. Look at me. I am a supervisor.... You could be a supervisor soon."[47]

Despite the supervisor's admonition, Constance declined the promotion, left the ODB, and enrolled at Columbia in February 1944. She was one of the first black women admitted to the law school.

"When I finally got to Columbia Law School the next February," she wrote, "I found—much to my surprise—that the student body included several other women like myself who were determined to become lawyers, notwithstanding the hard-nosed, antiwomen bias prevalent in the profession."[48] The dean of the law school had voted against admitting women, but once men were drafted into the army during World War II, women were viewed as acceptable candidates to fill the vacant seats at the law school.

Constance began working at the LDF as a law clerk in her second year of law school in October 1945. She accepted the position even though the dean and faculty at Columbia discouraged law students from having jobs because they considered the curriculum so demanding that students should devote all their time to their coursework. Ignoring the discouragement, Constance went to the LDF office, met its director counsel, Thurgood Marshall, and was delighted to get a job in a law office involved in civil rights litigation. She was especially pleased because a course in civil rights was not part of the curriculum at Columbia. The work as a law clerk gave her the opportunity to obtain the practical civil rights–related work experience that the law school curriculum did not. Once she began working on real cases at the LDF, Constance found law school to be "an unmitigated bore, wholly theoretical, esoteric, and without practical application."[49]

In June 1946 Constance Baker received her law degree, and two months later she married Joel Motley Jr.[50] Thanks to the financial assistance provided by Clarence Blakeslee, she had achieved her career goal. She had become a lawyer.

Blakeslee attended Constance's law school graduation ceremony. He congratulated her on her achievement and offered to help her find a job. He told her that he knew a Mr. Thacher at the Wall Street law firm of Simpson & Thacher and that he would be willing to see if Thacher, "who he believed to be a very fine man," would help her get a job. Constance had her heart set on civil rights work, however, so she thanked Blakeslee for his offer, politely declined, and informed him that she had secured a position at the LDF.[51]

Although they continued to correspond, this was the last time Constance ever saw Blakeslee. He died at the age of ninety-one in July 1954, less than two months after the Supreme Court rendered its decision in *Brown v. Board of Education*, a case on which Constance had worked as part of the LDF team. His death also occurred after she had become a primary actor in the battle to eradicate Jim Crow segregation, implement *Brown*, secure equal rights for blacks, and become the civil rights lawyer whom Southern segregationists referred to as "that Motley woman."[52]

After she passed the New York State bar examination, Constance Baker Motley became a full-time staff attorney at the LDF—the only civil rights law office she was aware of. For most of her career at the LDF, Motley was the only female lawyer.

An abundance of literature and numerous movie scripts and plays have been written about the LDF. They portray it as the oldest and the leading civil rights law firm in the country and credit it with winning more civil rights cases in the US Supreme Court than any other nongovernmental organization. The LDF won cases that ended de jure segregation in education, public accommodations, transportation, employment, and housing in addition to cases that protected black voting rights.

Much of the literature about the LDF primarily focuses on Thurgood Marshall, the director counsel of the LDF who subsequently became the first black Supreme Court justice, and other high-profile male lawyers who won civil rights cases, such as Charles Hamilton Houston, Robert Carter, Jack Greenberg, and James Nabrit Jr. Stories about Marshall present him as an American hero who systematically challenged segregation in the courts, won major desegregation cases, changed the law, and secured equal rights for blacks.

Although Marshall and the other men deserve credit for winning *Brown* and other important cases, Motley too was an LDF lawyer, and she actually went to the dangerous South, worked with local lawyers there, and tried many of the most significant desegregation cases that implemented *Brown*. Similar to other black women who played essential roles in the civil rights movement, she received less attention and less in-depth examination than the male lawyers. She was often completely omitted in stories or mentioned only in passing as contributing to the work of the men.

Some scholars have included Motley in their work. In addition, articles about her success in significant cases have appeared in local and regional Southern newspapers and in mostly black magazines such as *Ebony, Jet, Black Enterprise, Crisis*, and *Essence*. After her death, obituaries and articles about Motley appeared in major newspapers. Before her death, the only scholarly biographical work that explored her life and experiences in depth was written by Motley herself in 1988: *Equal Justice under Law: An Autobiography*.

4

Work in the Trenches

The Case-by-Case Implementation
of *Brown v. Board of Education*

One of the things I remember about my career in the 1950s and 1960s is being the only woman in the courtroom. . . . In the period 1949 to 1964, I tried school desegregation and other cases in eleven southern states and the District of Columbia and in that time I saw only one woman argue a case in the Fifth Circuit.
— Constance Baker Motley, quoted in J. Clay Smith Jr., *Rebels in Law: Voices in History of Black Women Lawyers*

We had, of course, anticipated that there would be resistance to implementation of the Supreme Court's decision in the *Brown* case. We had contemplated that opposition to the end of segregation would be felt, particularly in 1954, in the Deep South states—that is, Mississippi, Louisiana, Georgia, Alabama, South Carolina, and parts of Florida. We thought that there would be some resistance in Virginia, but not to the extent to which resistance actually developed in that state during the period 1954–1964. The one thing we did not foresee, however, was that federal troops would be utilized on more than one occasion to put down official resistance to the decision.
— Constance Baker Motley, "The Legacy of *Brown v. Board of Education*"

When Constance Baker Motley passed the bar exam and became a full-time staff attorney for the LDF, she entered a profession that was exclusionary and dominated primarily by white men. Both female lawyers and black lawyers, and especially black female lawyers, were almost nonexistent. Out of all the lawyers in the country at the time, only fifty-seven of them were black women.[1] Furthermore, very few female lawyers at that time did trial work in court.[2]

Motley was one of the first women to become a member of the New York City Bar Association. The first time she attempted to use its library she was stopped at the entrance by a white man—the gatekeeper—who initially ignored her while he continued a conversation with another white person. When he finally finished his lengthy conversation, he refused to permit Motley to enter the library, which he said was limited to members only. When she informed him that she was a member, he shouted in disbelief, "You are a member of this association?" Then he looked over the membership list, found her name, and said, "Oh, right this way, Constance."[3]

The LDF, like other civil rights organizations, was male-dominated when Motley began her work as a lawyer, and it remained that way throughout most of her career there. Despite that fact, she was not confined to the secretarial and other feminine roles that black women were relegated to in black churches and in the NAACP, the SCLC, and other national civil rights organizations. She became a key strategist and litigator and was assigned some of the most difficult desegregation cases—which she won. In the 1940s, that was an opportunity that very few female lawyers had.

Motley was at the forefront of the civil rights revolution. She was a lawyer with primary responsibility for trials to desegregate American society, case by case. She tried major desegregation cases in state and federal courts, took adverse decisions to courts of appeals, and was the first black woman to argue a case in the Supreme Court of the United States.

Motley was very comfortable, confident, and defiant in her role as a black woman challenging white lawyers, judges, and hostile witnesses in court as well as segregationist governors and other elected officials she encountered. She was also very secure about her situation as a woman working in a male-dominated environment. She had no doubt that she was as good at her craft as the male lawyers. Motley *was* good, and she wanted to look good when she argued her cases.

"Once a writer asked her what she did to prepare for her first argument in the Supreme Court," recalled her son, Joel Motley III, "and she replied, 'I went to Lord and Taylor and bought a new dress.' So she was able to kind of mix together a lot of different factors of being a woman and a successful lawyer at the same time."[4]

The victories Motley won in the courtroom affected the strategies and outcomes of the civil rights movement. They helped dismantle Jim Crow segregation, led to equality in many aspects of life for blacks and whites, and made both short-term and major long-term changes that helped transform the United States from a racist society to an inclusive and democratic society.

"During the civil rights movement, a lot of attention was given to the protests that were led by Dr. Martin Luther King . . . and freedom rides and the sit-ins," noted Drew S. Days III, a law professor at Yale, a former attorney at LDF, and a black lawyer who served as the US solicitor general under President Bill Clinton. "All of these got a lot of press, but it's important to remember that behind the scenes was a group of lawyers, mostly from the NAACP Legal Defense Fund, who dealt with the messiness from a legal standpoint of these activities. . . . When freedom riders were beaten up, when schoolchildren were expelled from school in Birmingham, it was Constance Motley and other lawyers from the Legal Defense Fund who went into court to try to get the courts to respond to those situations and make clear to the affected communities that the Constitution did not permit such action."[5]

Motley worked on a wide range of cases as a trial lawyer at the LDF. She not only excelled in cases involving the desegregation of colleges and universities in the South, she also won cases that ended the dual system of education altogether, forcing the desegregation of elementary, junior high, and senior high schools. She tried cases in eleven Southern states and in the District of Columbia, Ohio, New York, and New Jersey, and she was the counsel in hundreds of other LDF cases. The key to her leadership and agency in the civil rights movement was her work in the courts. She performed under very difficult circumstances; however, she was not afraid or deterred from doing her work. Rather, she exuded confidence and was eloquent and articulate; she was defiant and never hesitated to take difficult cases or to represent her clients in dangerous places.

Motley was widely admired for her style as an advocate. "She would appear to be indulgent to witnesses, appearing to allow them to get away with untrue statements, then turning on them with devastating effect," the *Guardian* reported.[6] Charlayne Hunter-Gault, one of Motley's former clients, witnessed this display of confidence, demeanor, and style in the courtroom when Motley represented her in the desegregation of the University of Georgia.

Thurgood Marshall, the director counsel of the LDF, sent Motley to Jackson, Mississippi, in 1948 to handle an equalization of salary lawsuit brought by black teachers against the city of Jackson and its public school system. That was the first big case that Motley tried. Robert Carter, a former federal judge in the Southern District of New York, a former general counsel of the NAACP, and a former attorney at the LDF, worked with her on the case.[7]

The black teachers were challenging the fact that they had systematically been paid less than white teachers even though they had better credentials than the white teachers. Most of the white teachers had bachelors degrees and had been educated in-state at the University of Mississippi. Most of the black teachers had masters degrees. Since colleges and universities in Mississippi were segregated, the black teachers had been forced to go out-of-state to pursue their higher education. They had obtained their degrees at New York University, the University of Chicago, and other institutions in the North and Midwest.[8]

Although the trial was held in Jackson, where Jim Crow was entrenched, the judge in the teachers' salary case was not a segregationist. He was from the more liberal Gulfport area of Mississippi rather than from the Jackson or Delta area, where blacks were severely oppressed and where the majority of whites were segregationists. He was also a federal judge who was appointed to the judiciary rather than a state court judge who was elected to his position. As a federal judge with a lifetime appointment, he was not concerned about reprisals from white voters if he was fair and ruled in favor of the teachers. He treated Motley and Carter with respect.[9]

The novelty of Motley, the first black female lawyer to try a case in a Mississippi courtroom, created a great deal of curiosity and excitement in the black community. "The whole town turned out to see the Negro lawyers from New York, one of whom was a woman," Motley noted.[10] She and the trial were also featured in the black media.[11]

Some blacks who lived in Mississippi were intimidated and afraid to challenge segregation; however, they worked past their fears and filled the courtroom every day of the trial.[12] On the first day, blacks arrived at the courthouse early. They didn't know whether the federal courtroom was segregated, but they did know that the state court was segregated. They therefore assumed that the federal court was segregated, too, so they all sat in the balcony or in the back of the court or stood along the walls if all the seats in the balcony and back had been taken by whites. At the end of the first day, Motley informed the blacks that the federal court was not segregated and that they could sit anywhere.

"When the case resumed the next morning at nine o'clock," said Motley, "all the seats were taken" by blacks, and the whites had to stand. Every day after the first day, "the blacks got to court early and took all the seats," said Motley.[13] The courtroom was packed every day until the trial ended. Motley remarked that it was, of course, something new for white people to experience. They had never before been in a situation where they had to stand and blacks were seated. In addition, they had never seen a black lawyer, and certainly not a black female lawyer, argue a case in court.

Derrick Bell, a former professor at New York University School of Law and Harvard Law School and a former attorney with the Civil Rights Division of the Justice Department, was Motley's colleague at the LDF and her assistant during the trial. He commented on the pride that black people took in her courtroom performance.

"The courts were crowded with black and white folk," he said. "White people on one side, black folks on the other, and the black people were just so proud of her. It didn't really matter to them whether she won or lost. . . . The fact that she was up there talking back to white folks was something that many of them had never done—could never do . . . so they were filled with pride. It's hard to convey the significance of black folk in those courts actually standing up—speaking out, arguing with, and disagreeing with white lawyers on the other side."[14]

At the beginning of the trial, Motley and Carter saw firsthand how fearful and submissive some black lawyers in the South were and why they would not assist the LDF in cases that challenged segregation. Those lawyers lived in the segregated communities in which they practiced law; they were subjected to repercussions that Motley and Carter were not subjected to because they returned to their homes in the North after the cases were over.

It was necessary for Motley and Carter to have a local attorney who was admitted to the Mississippi bar sign the complaint and receive service of all court papers. That was a huge problem because they were aware of only two black lawyers in the area, and one of them didn't want anything to do with the lawsuit. The other, a very elderly man who is known to us only as Burns, finally agreed to limited involvement with the case: he would file the complaint and accept service of papers for the LDF.[15]

Several unsettling things occurred during the trial. On the first day, Burns asked Motley and Carter to step outside the courtroom for a moment. When they got outside, he advised them, "Now, I think that you should address the white lawyers on the other side 'yes, suh' and 'no, suh.'" When Carter asked why he and Motley should do this, Burns replied, "Because I think you'll prejudice the case if you don't say, 'yes, suh' and 'no, suh' to them." Carter responded, "No, we're not going to say that. The case will just have to be prejudiced."[16]

There were some awkward moments in the courtroom when the federal judge had trouble addressing Motley. He was not accustomed to using the title *Mrs.* when speaking to trial lawyers. In 1949 there were few female trial lawyers in the United States, and apparently none had appeared in his court in Mississippi. The local newspapers also had a problem when referring to Motley in their stories about the trial. Rather than identifying her as Mrs. Motley, a visiting lawyer from New York, they referred to her derisively as "that Motley woman."[17]

One thing that particularly disturbed Motley was the mural in the federal courtroom where the trial was held. It depicted life in Mississippi and included an antebellum mansion scene with elegantly dressed white people. The women wore long gowns and hats and held parasols. Standing next to the whites were black people, presumably slaves, with bales of cotton. Motley found the mural ironic and offensive, especially since it depicted the very system she was challenging: a white supremacist policy that set blacks apart and treated them as inferior.[18]

Finding a place to stay while they were litigating the case was also challenging. Hotels in Mississippi were segregated, so Motley and Carter could not stay in them. Blacks in Jackson were intimidated and oppressed by whites and were therefore not willing to have Motley and Carter stay in their homes. They had grown up in a state of fear—an actual fear of reprisals by the white community for any effort at all that seemed to challenge the system of discrimination. Most blacks were also dependent on the white community for their jobs and well being.

Black visitors to Mississippi and other places in the South usually stayed with relatives or friends.[19] While they were in Jackson, however, Motley and Carter stayed in a black-owned motel that had minimal furnishing and a stove in the same room they slept and ate in.[20] The accommodations were typical of those available in the South for black traveling salesmen.

Lunch counters and restaurants were also segregated in Mississippi, so there was no place near the court for Motley and Carter to eat during the trial. Most lunch counters, restaurants, hotels, and other public accommodations in the South remained racially segregated until Congress passed (and the president signed) the Civil Rights Act of 1964.[21]

One day for lunch, Carter and Motley went into a local grocery store down the street from the court. The white man who owned the store completely ignored them. He didn't acknowledge their presence until he had completed a very long conversation with a white customer.

"Finally," Motley recalled, "he said to Bob [Carter], 'What do you want, boy?' and in that moment . . . I realized for the first time—how humiliating it was for a black man to have to say, 'I'll take a few apples' and not being able to say, 'I'm not a boy.'" Describing the anger she felt, Motley added, "I kind of bristled, and both of us knew I was bristling, and he [Carter] said, 'Don't say anything.' And so we got our fruit and he hustled me out of there."[22] In her autobiography she wrote, "I felt Bob's hand pulling me out the door. I melted in anger. It's a good thing I was not a candle."[23]

The immediate and long-term impact of Motley's work in the teacher salary case was tremendous. Equal pay for teachers was an important issue that affected the entire black community in Jackson and the state of Mississippi. One of the reasons it was an important issue was that teachers were among the few blacks in the community who had a regular income and economic viability. The only others were black barbers, beauticians, undertakers, doctors, preachers, and a few who were self-employed and independent of the white community.

Although their salaries were lower than those paid to white teachers, black teachers enjoyed some aspects of middle-class status. They were able to purchase nice homes, cars, televisions, and things that average black people in Mississippi could not buy. The theory in the black community was that if black teachers were paid more money, everybody in the black community would benefit, because the teachers would have more money to give to black churches and spend in black businesses.[24]

Another case that Motley worked on shortly after she became a full-time staff attorney at the LDF was *Sweatt v. Painter* in 1950.[25] The plaintiff, Herman Marion Sweatt, a black man, applied for admission to the University of Texas Law School. After he was rejected on the basis of race, Sweatt filed a lawsuit against the university. The LDF successfully represented him in the action and obtained a judgment that forced the university to admit him.

Yet even though the university admitted Sweatt, it applied the "separate but equal" standard of the 1896 *Plessy v. Ferguson* case and "hurriedly established a separate law school for blacks—in effect, just for him" in the basement of a building in Austin, Texas.[26] In addition to being established in an inferior building, the all-black law school had significantly fewer books in its library, fewer pro-fessors on its staff, and fewer programs (such as moot court and externship op-portunities).

Sweatt was one of many education desegregation cases of the LDF's legal strategy to challenge the Supreme Court's ruling in *Plessy*. The strategy, which had been developed by the NAACP in the 1920s and 1930s, focused on school integration, housing, voting rights, and employment discrimination.

Initially the NAACP focused on the desegregation of professional and gradu-ate schools because of two beliefs: that there would be less white resistance to the admission of blacks to higher education and that it would not be as difficult to prove to a court that the few black students who had been rejected from graduate schools were as qualified as the white students who had been admitted.[27] In 1935 the plan worked. The LDF prevailed in *Gaines v. Missouri* when the Supreme Court ruled that Missouri could not provide in-state education for whites to at-tend law school and send blacks out-of-state to attend law school.[28]

After its victory in *Gaines*, the NAACP and the LDF lawyers began looking for test cases to challenge segregated school systems in the South and to attack the constitutionality of "separate but equal" and of racial segregation in public education. They found five cases and took them to the Supreme Court, where they were consolidated into *Brown v. Board of Education*. Motley was part of the legal team that won that historic desegregation case.

When one thinks of how Jim Crow was dismantled and how desegregation became a reality, *Brown*, the landmark US Supreme Court case, usually comes to mind. The court's order directing schools to desegregate and admit blacks was momentous; however, it was not automatically implemented. Resistance to the ruling was widespread, especially in the Deep South. The authorities in those states were angered by *Brown* and refused to comply with the court's order to admit black students to the all-white schools.

The ruling enraged white segregationists on the local, state, and even the na-tional level. In fact, a few weeks after the Supreme Court's decision, "James O. Eastland from Mississippi stood on the Senate floor and declared, 'Let me make this very clear. The South will retain segregation!'"[29]

Eastland's emphatic declaration encouraged defiant rhetoric and acts of re-sistance to the implementation of *Brown* by white segregationist governors, leg-islators, school boards, lawyers, and even judges. Their inflammatory statements and defiant acts encouraged the fight to maintain racially segregated schools and racially segregated lunch counters, recreational facilities, bus terminals, hotels, and other public accommodations.[30]

Blacks in the South soon realized that the struggle had just begun—that state and local governments across the South were determined to resist the implemen-tation of *Brown* and large-scale desegregation in the United States. Rather than integrate the schools, state and local officials created obstacles and blockades to ensure strategies of delay, avoidance, and resistance. As a result of the resistance, the LDF was deluged with desegregation cases.

The plaintiffs in *Brown* had challenged the application of the "separate but equal" doctrine established in *Plessy* to public school education. The latter case had involved a challenge to a Louisiana statute that required railroad companies to provide separate accommodations for blacks and whites. "Separate but equal" became the law of the land when the Supreme Court upheld the Louisiana law and ruled that separate facilities for blacks and whites were constitutional.

The court's ruling in *Plessy* put the imprimatur of the United States on legal segregation. It sanctioned racial segregation in public accommodations, education, and most other aspects of life. Motley criticized the decision, which gave a ringing endorsement to the establishment of separate societies for blacks and whites and established the United States as a racist society. She expressed her opinion of the court's ruling as follows:

> Our Supreme Court recognized, early on, that, although some Africans had been enslaved by Europeans and American colonists, non-enslaved Africans were among the free peoples of the world. This explicit recognition of free Africans as free people occurred in 1841 in the *Amistad* case. In 1857, however, when asked to determine the status of free Africans in the American community, the Supreme Court noted that our Founding Fathers never contemplated that free Africans would constitute a part of the body politic. The high court said, in dicta, that free Africans in American society had always been regarded as an inferior order of beings and had no rights that a white man was bound to respect. Thus, the Court plainly established the young United States as a racist society.[31]

When questioned about her opinion that the court's decision established the United States as a racist society, Motley responded, "If the court's decision had gone the other way, it's clear we would not have had a society which developed as completely segregated as it did with the sanction of law. That decision affected not only public institutions but private institutions as well."[32]

On May 17, 1954, the court issued its landmark ruling in *Brown*. It held that the doctrine of "separate but equal" had no place in the field of public education and that separate educational facilities were inherently unequal. The case became known as *Brown I*.[33] The court did not prescribe any remedy for desegregating public schools in *Brown I*. It did, however, subsequently order public school desegregation to begin in a case decided the next year: *Brown II*. It sent the five consolidated cases back to the lower courts and ordered them to use traditional equity principles to provide remedies to desegregate public schools and to admit black children to them on a "racially nondiscriminatory basis with *all deliberate speed*."[34]

Throughout the country, many blacks applauded the ruling; they were optimistic about the end of racism and de jure (legal) segregation after the *Brown* decision reversed a constitutional trend that had been validated in *Plessy*. They believed that the ruling marked the beginning of the end of Jim Crow.[35] However, Southern blacks who had lived in the system of segregation for decades were not as optimistic. They were not so naive to believe that Southern white segregationists would suddenly change just because the Supreme Court had issued a desegregation order.

It soon became patently clear to all that the end of Jim Crow racism would be agonizingly slow in becoming a reality, since segregationists vehemently denounced the ruling and states in the South refused to comply with the court's order to admit black children to all-white schools.[36] Opposition to the desegregation order spread throughout the South, and by the end of 1956 eleven Southern states had passed 106 prosegregation measures. Nineteen senators and eighty-two members of the House of Representatives from Southern states—including the entire congressional delegations from Alabama, Arkansas, Georgia, Louisiana, Mississippi, South Carolina, and Virginia—signed the Southern Manifesto on Integration, a document written by Senator Strom Thurmond of South Carolina. The manifesto opposed the racial integration of public places, denounced attempts to force integration on the South, "stirred Confederate pride," and promoted efforts to reverse *Brown*.[37] In Tennessee, Texas, Kentucky, West Virginia, and Arkansas, mobs of white segregationists attempted to block black students from entering some of the first Southern schools to be desegregated.[38]

The LDF was flooded with school desegregation cases as a result of the defiance and hostility of segregationist school board officials and governors who used their power to prevent the implementation of *Brown*. The LDF had to hurriedly come up with a strategy to desegregate schools. Motley became an integral part of the strategy that was devised. She was assigned some of the most significant education desegregation cases and was sent to dangerous places all over the South to try them.[39]

It was the work in the trenches—trying those cases in state after state, city after city, and school district after school district to enforce the court's ruling—that actually implemented *Brown* and desegregated America. Motley's action and agency mattered. Without the victories she won in the courtroom, public schools, colleges, and universities might not have been desegregated, and the goals of the movement might not have been achieved. Motley worked under difficult and often dangerous conditions. She experienced racial insults from segregationist school officials, governors, and even judges in her work to implement *Brown*. She "endured gawking [and] physical threats" and was "often accosted by hostile white spectators in the corridors of Southern courts or outside on the side-walk."[40] In Alabama and Mississippi local black leaders had to surround her with bodyguards armed with machine guns out of fear that she would be attacked and killed. Black men armed with machine guns also escorted her during the day and stood on rooftops and outside houses where she slept at night to protect her.[41]

In the aftermath of *Brown II*, the Little Rock, Arksansas, school board ap-proved a desegregation plan. It called for desegregation of grades ten through twelve, beginning in 1957. Daisy Bates, the president of the Little Rock NAACP, initiated and led the effort to end the dual school system and implement the plan.[42] She identified and recruited black students to integrate Central High School. On August 27, 1957, when the plan was to go into effect, the Mothers' League, a group of segregationist parents, filed a lawsuit to prevent desegrega-tion. It obtained a temporary injunction barring the school board from moving forward with the plan.

Issues of race and politics intersected with efforts to desegregate public schools in Little Rock. The governor, Orval Faubus, was seeking reelection. He figured that it would be politically advantageous for him to support the Mothers' League lawsuit, oppose integration of the schools, and endear himself to the white elec-torate in order to be elected to another term. On September 2, 1957, the day be-fore school was to open, Faubus went on radio and television and announced to the citizens of Little Rock that he had deployed the Arkansas National Guard to Central High to physically block the black students from entering the building.[43]

About two weeks before Faubus's announcement, Judge Ronald N. Davies had been temporarily transferred from the District Court for the District of North Dakota to the District Court for the Eastern District of Arkansas, which was located in Little Rock. On August 30, 1957, Davies nullified the injunction the Mothers' League had obtained and ordered the school board to implement the plan to desegregate the schools. Despite the court order, Faubus deployed the Arkansas National Guard to prevent the black students from entering Central High. The situation became quite tense when Daisy Bates and nine black stu-dents attempted to enter the building and register at the beginning of the school year in September. They were met by an angry mob of white parents, who were accompanied by the troops Faubus had sent to block the students' entrance.[44]

The LDF went to court to obtain an order to force the school to admit the students. Motley and Jack Greenberg, a Columbia University Law School pro-fessor and former vice dean and the former director counsel of the LDF, con-stantly commuted from New York to Little Rock to take depositions, interview witnesses, and prepare the case, which (along with the students involved) became known as the Little Rock Nine. Wiley Branton, a black attorney in Arkansas, worked with Motley and Greenberg as local counsel in the case.[45]

On three different occasions Judge Davies ordered the school board to proceed with the implementation of the desegregation plan (his first two orders were ignored). On September 20, 1957, he issued an order enjoining Faubus from using the National Guard to interfere with the students' entrance of Central High. Three days later, on September 23, the students entered the school through a side door; however, they were quickly whisked away when an enraged white mob realized they were in the building, rioted, and threatened to kill one of them.[46]

The situation became so volatile and dangerous that President Dwight Eisenhower was forced to nationalize the Arkansas National Guard into active duty and station troops at Central High to enforce Judge Davies's order and protect the nine students from the angry mob. On September 24 the National Guard, supplemented by one thousand paratroopers from the 101st Airborne Division from Fort Campbell, Kentucky, was dispatched to Little Rock. The soldiers stood guard and surrounded the black students as they entered the building through the front door the next day, September 25.[47] On May 27, 1958, Ernest Green became the first black student to graduate from Central High School.

Carlotta Walls LaNier, the youngest member of the Little Rock Nine, described the students' struggle to enter Central High and how she first met Motley, "the only woman attorney in a smoke-filled room with the other male lawyers" who worked with Daisy Bates in the legal battle to desegregate the school.[48] When Motley was in Little Rock to represent the LDF, she stayed with Bates.[49]

LaNier described the scene when she and the other students finally entered the school: "under the protection of the federal troops, a convoy of jeeps" and with "soldiers dressed in helmets and combat gear with rifles drawn."[50]

The protracted battle to desegregate Central High was followed by many, many more school desegregation cases. It sent searing messages to the NAACP, the LDF, and blacks throughout the South about the strength of segregationist opposition to *Brown* and school integration.

Although the Little Rock Nine eventually entered and enrolled in the school with the assistance of President Eisenhower's reluctant intervention, the desegregation of Central High School "never became a clear-cut victory for the NAACP," and Faubus's landslide reelection to another term as governor of Arkansas "highlighted the fervor" of the resistance and opposition to integration. "Historian Adam Fairclough affirmed that Little Rock foreshadowed years of dogged white resistance that not only delayed large-scale integration for more than a decade, but also ensured that the all-white schools were eventually integrated under the worst possible circumstances," Francoise Hamlin wrote.[51]

Motley was the LDF lawyer assigned to litigate many of the cases that resulted in the integration of all-white public schools under the worst possible circumstances. After Thurgood Marshall left the LDF in 1961 to take a seat on the Second Circuit Court of Appeals, Motley inherited many of his cases and assumed primary responsibility for the campaign to use the legal system to desegregate America.[52] With the assistance of local counsel, she tried cases to enforce the ruling in *Brown*. Derrick Bell, an LDF attorney who worked closely with her on desegregation cases, commented that her job was made much harder, especially when the school board members and governors were elected officials who for political reasons resisted trial court orders to desegregate schools.[53] They wanted to prevent the *Brown* decision from being enforced in their state because they did not want to appear to be friendly to blacks and alienate their white constituents.

The defiance and refusal to comply with *Brown* required Motley to file and litigate desegregation cases throughout the South; she had to file lawsuit after lawsuit. When she won a case in the trial court and obtained an order to desegregate the schools, the Southern state that lost to her would appeal the ruling; therefore, in addition to arguing desegregation cases on the trial level, she was constantly busy opposing state petitions in appellate courts and trying to sustain the victories (favorable rulings) she had won in the lower courts.

It was a daunting task for Motley to litigate case after case. She had to leave her family in the North, make constant trips to the South, and spend extended periods away from her family challenging hostile school boards, university and college administrators, and even segregationist judges to win the cases. She also had to fight governors, mayors, and angry mobs of citizens who opposed integration and adopted tactics to block black students when they attempted to enter and enroll in all-white schools.

In court Motley won the desegregation cases on issues of law; however, there was still persistent racism that prevented the victories from actually being implemented. The cases she won to force the University of Alabama to admit Autherine Lucy, the University of Mississippi to admit James Meredith, and the University of Georgia to admit Charlayne Hunter and Hamilton Holmes are examples of the persistent racism and resistance she encountered. Motley persevered and prevailed against all three universities in the trial courts; however, she had to return to the courts time after time to appeal to higher federal courts, including the Supreme Court, to obtain orders to implement the victories and remove hostile governors who stood in doorways and used state police to prevent black students from entering the buildings and enrolling. She also had to endure personal taunts and threats of physical violence from segregationist mobs to actually get the black students into the universities.

Motley's job was made particularly difficult because of the hostility and resistance of two segregationist governors who were vehemently opposed to the integration of schools and universities in their states: George Wallace, the governor of Alabama, and Ross Barnett, the governor of Mississippi. Federal courts had ordered Wallace to permit Autherine Lucy to enroll at the University of Alabama. Federal courts had also ordered Barnett to permit James Meredith to enroll at the University of Mississippi. Both governors refused to comply with the desegregation order. At that point Motley's work shifted into high gear, and she became involved in what have become known as the trigger points for resistance, hostility, and violence in the civil rights movement.[54] She became the lead attorney, and with the assistance of local counsel, she fought the battle and won the cases to desegregate the universities.

The period in history characterized as the Black People's Awakening coincided with the Montgomery Bus Boycott and Motley's representation of Autherine Lucy in her lawsuit to be admitted to the University of Alabama. Both events occurred in the aftermath of *Brown* and led to a great deal of white resistance in Alabama.[55]

In 1952, after graduating with a BA in English from Miles College, an all-black institution in Alabama, twenty-six-year-old Autherine Lucy filed her application to enroll as a graduate student at the all-white University of Alabama at Tuscaloosa.[56] The application was denied because of the university's racially discriminatory admission policy, and Lucy sought assistance from the NAACP.

On June 29, 1955, Motley, Marshall, and Arthur Shores, local counsel in Alabama, obtained a court order to force the university to admit Lucy. Judge Harlan Hobart Grooms in the District Court for the Northern District of Alabama issued the order and permanently enjoined the university from denying Lucy's application on the basis of race.[57] A few days later, he amended the order to apply to all black students who applied for admission to the university.

Judge Grooms's order was upheld by the Supreme Court on October 10, 1955. In a unanimous decision, the court ordered the University of Alabama to admit Lucy.[58] As with other school desegregation cases, however, winning in the courts was just the beginning of the battle to desegregate the university.

The University of Alabama reluctantly complied with the court's order and admitted Lucy as its first black student. It permitted her to register as a graduate student in library science; however, it barred her from living in any of the all-white dormitories or eating in the all-white cafeteria.[59]

Lucy enrolled and began attending classes on February 1, 1956. When she appeared on campus a few days later, she was met by a hostile mob that was determined to keep her from attending classes. The enraged white mob surrounded her and shouted "Keep 'Bama white," "Where is the nigger?", and "Lynch her!"

Mob violence and a riot broke out, and the police were called to restore order. After a three-hour siege of the classroom building in which the violent mob had trapped Lucy, the university expelled her. It alleged that she had caused the riot, that "the threat of violence was too great for the school to handle," and that it could not provide protection for her.[60]

Motley quickly traveled back to Alabama, went to court, and filed a petition seeking to have Lucy reinstated. She argued that "Lucy was not the source of the problem and that she should be readmitted." The case went dormant when Lucy decided not to pursue readmission because of threats on her life, the mob violence directed against her, and the lack of protection by the federal government.[61]

Motley was disappointed with the failure of the federal government to step in and provide protection for Lucy and to support her efforts to implement *Brown*. She expressed her opinion about the inaction of the president and the Justice Department as follows:

> Eisenhower was president in the Lucy case, and that was one of the reasons the suit was abandoned, because Eisenhower and the Justice Department were not on our side and were not backing us with respect to the resistance offered by the people in Alabama. . . . This was one of the things that the federal judge discussed with us, that there's no protection. . . . 'Who's going to protect her down there?' The president was not going to call out federal troops to protect her, the state was not going to protect her, and the local police who had stood by when the riots occurred may have been leaders of the Ku Klux Klan, so there was real danger in sending Lucy back to the University of Alabama.[62]

Shortly after the *Lucy* case was filed in 1955, resistance to integration reached its peak; anger and turmoil erupted when another explosive development occurred in Montgomery, Alabama. Jo Ann Gibson Robinson, an English professor at Alabama State College and the president of the Women's Political Council (WPC), and the members of the WPC spontaneously initiated the Montgomery Bus Boycott to protest the treatment of blacks and the policy of racial discrimination on the city's public buses.

Each bus in Montgomery had thirty-six seats; the front ten rows of double seats were reserved exclusively for whites, and the seats in the back were for blacks. The objectionable policy required blacks who were seated to get up and give their seats to whites when the driver instructed them to do so. It also required blacks to stand when there were no vacant seats in the black section of the bus even if all the seats in the section reserved for whites were empty.[63] Blacks were required to pay their bus fare at the front of the bus and then get off and walk to the back of the bus and reenter through the side door. Sometimes the white bus driver would drive off after black passengers had paid their fare but before they reached the side door, "leaving them standing in the street." The white drivers were also quite rude to black passengers; they treated them with contempt and referred to them as "niggers, black cows, and black apes."[64]

The lawsuit to desegregate the University of Alabama and the Montgomery Bus Boycott occurred within a year of the ruling in *Brown*. Both were catalytic events in the civil rights movement, and both were initiated by black women.

Recent scholarly literature provides evidence that black women were often the spark that ignited a number of the civil rights movement's most prominent protests, demonstrations, and activities that historians have described as being led by black men when in fact they were led by black women.[65] The Montgomery Bus Boycott was an example. After black women had initiated, organized, and sustained the boycott, black men—primarily ministers—stepped in, took over, and became publicly acknowledged as the leaders.

Robinson and the WPC should be credited with leading the boycott. They had planned it long before Dr. Martin Luther King Jr., his good friend and civil rights leader Reverend Ralph Abernathy, and other black ministers got involved. The women were motivated to act because of the objectionable seating policy and other abuses suffered by blacks who rode city buses in Montgomery. They were appalled by two incidents in particular: a young black man had been shot in the back by the police for simply talking back to a bus driver, and two black children who were visiting from New Jersey had been arrested after they refused to give up their seats to a white man and boy.[66]

"Jo Ann had been advocating desegregation of the buses before the black ministers stepped in," Bernard Lafayette Jr. recalled. "However, when you called a mass meeting and the press got involved, men got the credit because they spoke at the public rallies. . . . Jo Ann took the initiative, organized the women, and continued the Montgomery Bus Boycott while the preachers were in a meeting at the church arguing over what to do next."[67]

The women had filed a written complaint with Montgomery's mayor about the policy that required blacks to surrender their seats to white bus passengers and warned that they would organize a boycott of the buses if the policy was not changed. While they were finalizing their boycott plans, Claudette Colvin, a fifteen-year-old black girl, was handcuffed, physically dragged off a city bus, arrested, and jailed because of her refusal to get out of her seat and give it to a white passenger.[68] Colvin was an unmarried and pregnant teenager. Because of her out-of-wedlock pregnancy and the negative portrayal of black women's sexuality, the black establishment and religious community in Montgomery determined that she could not be the standard bearer for this protest action.[69]

Anger and outrage over Colvin's physical abuse and arrest was still simmering on December 1, 1955, when Rosa Parks, the secretary of the Montgomery NAACP chapter, was arrested. She too had refused to get up, give her seat on the bus to a white person, and move to the back of the bus.[70]

As word of Parks's arrest spread, Robinson sprang into action and put the WPC's plan into effect. She immediately launched the boycott and encouraged blacks in Montgomery to stay off the buses until the discriminatory seating policy was abandoned.

Robinson drafted, mimeographed, and distributed more than thirty-five thousand handbills to the black residents of Montgomery. She alerted them about Parks's arrest, and she urged them to boycott the buses in protest and to demand an end to the discriminatory policy toward blacks.[71]

Initially the boycott was supposed to last only one day, while Parks was on trial. However, at the end of that day the boycott had proved to be so successful that Robinson decided to continue it. Throughout the duration of the boycott, she produced a newsletter and distributed leaflets to keep the black community fully informed about the protest action. She and the other women of the WPC were change agents, not only in initiating and organizing the boycott but also in sustaining it to its successful conclusion. National, regional, and local media covered the boycott, and mass meetings were held at churches and other venues.

King and other black ministers and community leaders in Montgomery joined the boycott and protest action, formed the Montgomery Improvement Association (MIA) on December 5, 1955, and worked with Robinson and the WPC as well as with Fred Gray, the attorney for the bus boycott, to achieve their goals: a first-come, first-served seating policy on the buses; courteous treatment of blacks on the buses; and employment of black bus drivers on the bus routes in predominantly black neighborhoods.[72]

The entire black community rallied in response to Robinson's call for action; everyone supported the boycott and refused to ride the city buses. Some people rode bicycles, organized car pools, and used other means of transportation to go to church, to go to school, to shop, and to go about their other daily activities. Others, young and old, just walked wherever they needed to go. Some white families picked up their domestic workers and drove them to work.

The bus company lost revenue because of the boycott; white businesses in Montgomery also lost revenue because their black customers refused to ride the buses to patronize them. Enraged whites retaliated against blacks who participated in the boycott. Some blacks were victims of individual acts of violence, and others were attacked by mobs of angry whites.

The boycott established a new form of racial protest—the mobilization of local citizens for a mass movement—and ignited the civil rights movement. It also provided speaking opportunities, extensive media coverage, and national attention for King and led to him being appointed as the president of the MIA.[73] As soon as he became the "newly appointed president" of the MIA, King "delivered his first speech on the bus boycott. An overflow crowd of thousands . . . spilled out of the church and into the streets. Outdoor speakers were set up to enable all in attendance to hear the first address of the young and emerging leader," a black minister who became the recognized spokesman for the MIA and the recognized leader of the boycott.[74]

The work the black women performed in the early phase of the boycott allowed the men to join the protest activity and ascend to formal leadership of an already mobilized constituency and movement. When the men stepped in, they took over. Robinson and the women of the WPC did not have the same status, influence, power, or access to resources that the men had. As a result they were forced to recede to the background. The men, who as (mostly) ministers were very charismatic speakers, made speeches to overflow crowds at rallies and mass meetings and became perceived by the civil rights community, the public, the media, and historians as the leaders of the boycott.

Alabama had adopted an antiboycott law in 1921. When one hundred blacks were indicted under that law for participating in the bus boycott, Motley and the LDF filed an action challenging the constitutionality of the law.[75] The boycott continued, lasting 382 days. Motley's representation of Lucy in her lawsuit to desegregate the University of Alabama, together with the challenge to the antiboycott law and the continuation of the bus boycott, further inflamed segregationists in Alabama.

A successful resolution of the boycott was achieved in November 1956 when the Supreme Court issued a ruling in which it held that racial segregation of buses in Montgomery was unconstitutional. It affirmed the decision of the district court of Alabama, which found that "the statutes and ordinances requiring segregation of the white and colored races on the motor buses of a common carrier of passengers in the City of Montgomery and its police jurisdiction violated the due process and equal protection of the law clauses of the Fourteenth Amendment to the Constitution of the United States."[76] The boycott ended only after the court ruled that segregation in public transportation was illegal and the bus company abandoned its policy of forcing black passengers to surrender their seats to whites and agreed to hire black drivers for routes in predominantly black neighborhoods.

The mass demonstrations and national media coverage of the nonviolent direct action that led to the successful end of the boycott were significant in establishing Martin Luther King Jr. as a recognized leader of the civil rights movement. They were also significant in the recognition of the organization that was officially named the Southern Christian Leadership Conference in August 1957, almost a year after the successful conclusion of the boycott.[77]

In May 1963 James Hood and Vivian Malone, two young black adults, applied for admission to the University of Alabama. Their applications were denied, and they too went to the LDF for assistance. Motley became their lawyer and added them as plaintiffs to the *Lucy* case, which had been filed against the university in 1955 and was still pending.

On May 21, 1963, Judge Harlan Grooms—the same judge who had ordered the university to admit Lucy approximately seven years earlier—ordered the university to enroll Hood and Malone. As soon as the order was issued, George Wallace, the politically ambitious governor of Alabama, announced that he would prevent Hood and Malone from entering the university. President John F. Kennedy responded with a proclamation commanding Wallace and all others in Alabama to cease and desist from actions to obstruct justice. The president also ordered the secretary of defense to take all necessary and appropriate action to enforce the laws of the United States in Alabama to ensure that the court order was carried out.

Despite the president's proclamation, when Hood and Malone attempted to register on June 11, 1963, "Wallace stood in the doorway at the entrance to Foster Auditorium on the campus of the University of Alabama in Tuscaloosa" and attempted to block them from entering. His obstructive action forced President Kennedy to federalize the Alabama National Guard to escort the two students back to the campus later that day. After a brief confrontation with US Deputy Attorney General Nicholas Katzenbach, Wallace stepped aside, and the two black students proceeded to enter the building, "flanked by the guard now under the president's control" and enroll as students at the University of Alabama.[78]

The hostility and danger that Motley was exposed to in Alabama when the bus boycott and *Lucy* trial converged, and when she represented Hood and Maloney, provide some indication of how she experienced the civil rights movement as she performed her work as a trial lawyer in the South. The possibility existed that she could be killed, particularly at night while she slept.

Motley and Marshall stayed at the home of Arthur Shores while working in Montgomery. The hotels were segregated so they had no other place to stay. Shores worked as the local counsel with Marshall, Motley, and the LDF on desegregation cases in Alabama. He was the only black lawyer in Alabama from 1937 to 1947. Other blacks became lawyers in Alabama in the early 1950s.

Although Shores had a beautiful home and made Motley feel very welcome in it, she always stayed awake all night there. She couldn't sleep because his house had been bombed more than fifteen times in the 1950s and early 1960s.[79] Whenever she was in Shores's home, black men armed with machine guns and rifles were always outside the garage and on the roof; they also patrolled the sidewalk to provide protection. Local black leaders "surrounded Motley and Marshall with armed bodyguards out of fear that the famous lawyers would be attacked." The armed men never left; they rotated in shifts around the clock to protect the house while the lawyers were inside. The fear that Motley and Marshall could be harmed was especially high among those in the black community because King's house had also been firebombed.[80]

Almost everybody Motley associated with in Alabama carried a gun to protect her. Even Arthur Shores's secretary, who met Motley at the airport, carried a gun in a little brown bag, which she inadvertently left on the airline counter one day. As Motley and the secretary were about to get in her car and leave the airport, the secretary exclaimed, "Oh, my goodness, I have to go back and get my bag." Motley thought the bag had a sandwich in it, so she suggested that the secretary should just leave it. The secretary responded, "No, I have my gun in there." That's when Motley realized that Shores, his secretary, and the black men who guarded his house while she was inside all carried guns to provide protection for her while she was in Alabama.[81]

Motley's name is associated with the desegregation of the University of Georgia, and she won a similar case against Georgia State College. The judge ruled in her favor in that case, and blacks enrolled there for the first time. As with other cases, her experiences in the desegregation of educational institutions in Georgia were not fully examined by historians.

Motley persevered in the fight to implement the goals of the civil rights movement when she successfully represented Charlayne Hunter and Hamilton Holmes in their lawsuit against the University of Georgia after their applications for admission had been denied for disingenuous reasons.[82] The lawsuit was filed in 1959, and Donald Hollowell, a local LDF attorney in Atlanta, was part of Motley's team in the case. Charlayne Hunter-Gault later shared her memories of how Motley's advocacy forced the desegregation of the university and how she participated in that experience with her.

"When I was seventeen years old and a senior at the Henry McNeal Turner High School in Atlanta," Hunter-Gault recalled, "a group of aggressive black leaders in Atlanta came to my school and wanted to know if there were any students who might be qualified to enter a white institution and would be interested in doing it." That institution was Georgia State College. Because of a previous unsuccessful attempt to desegregate the college, the black leaders were looking for what they called two squeaky clean kids. "Hamilton was the high school football captain and I was the high school football queen," Hunter-Gault continued. "He was brilliant and turned out to be first in the class of 156 and I was third, so we were the squeaky clean kids they were looking for."

"Hamilton and I went to . . . Georgia State," which was in downtown Atlanta, so the black leaders knew the two students could be protected from whatever racial situations or violence might arise there. "When we got down there and looked at the curriculum at Georgia State, we . . . looked at each other and said, 'This isn't good enough,'" said Hunter-Gault. "I remember to this day, we walked out of the Georgia State office of the registrar, and the adults who had taken us there were devastated because we said, 'Uh-uh, this is not going to work.' And then Hamilton . . . pointed north, and we all knew without him even saying it that he meant the University of Georgia" in Athens. The adults who had taken them to Georgia State said, "Oh no"—the University of Georgia was not in or near downtown Atlanta, and there was no plan in place to protect them there. "We didn't know anybody in Athens," Hunter-Gault stated. "There was no network to support us there, and it was Klan territory."[83]

Despite the protestations and expressions of concern from the black leaders who had recruited them to apply to Georgia State College, Hunter and Holmes applied to the University of Georgia because of the superior academics there. Hunter wanted to take courses that would prepare her to become a journalist; Holmes wanted to take courses that would prepare him to become a physician. When their applications for admission were denied, the LDF took their case to force the university to admit them. Motley was assigned as their attorney. She worked with local counsel and handled the entire case, including the drafting and filing of all documents in court, the discovery of information necessary to win the case, the examination of witnesses, and the oral arguments in all hearings in all phases of the case. Motley was required to stay in Georgia for extended periods throughout the litigation. While the case was pending, Hunter enrolled at Wayne State University in Detroit, and she traveled to Georgia whenever she was needed to participate in the trial.

Vernon Jordan Jr. also worked on the case. Jordan—whose stellar career would include being an advisor to President Bill Clinton, the director of the NAACP, the executive director of the United Negro College Fund, and the president of the National Urban League— graduated from Howard Law School in June 1960 and obtained his dream job: the position of law clerk for Donald Hollowell, at a salary of $35 a week.[84] Because he was working for Hollowell, who was a local LDF lawyer, Jordan was also working for Motley on the case to desegregate the University of Georgia.

The trial took place in the federal district court in Macon, Georgia. Judge William Augustus Bootle, the trial judge, ruled that Hunter and Holmes were fully qualified for immediate admission and that they would have been admitted had it not been for their race.[85]

On January 6, 1961, Bootle ordered the University of Georgia to admit Hunter and Holmes. The state moved for a stay of the order, and Bootle granted the motion. Motley immediately filed a petition to vacate the stay. She went to the Fifth Circuit Court of Appeals in Atlanta and argued her case before Judge Elbert Tuttle. Hollowell accompanied her to the court of appeals, where Tuttle granted the petition.[86]

Governmental officials in Georgia were hostile and opposed to desegregation of the university, so Motley had to fight them in addition to the university officials to get Hunter and Holmes admitted. After she won the case, the officials threatened to close the university rather than permit Hunter and Holmes to enroll and desegregate it. That action prompted a ninety-mile-an-hour car race between the Georgia attorney general and Motley as she rushed to the court of appeals in Atlanta to have a judge there sign her papers so she could appeal the case to the Supreme Court.

"I remember when we went to Atlanta," Motley recalled. "Attorney General Cook was driving his car because he knew we were going to Atlanta and appeal. . . .

And so he was driving with his associates at 90 miles an hour, and we were right behind him. We figured they'd have to arrest him first before they arrested us, and we all got to Atlanta about noon."[87] The next day, after the court heard the appeal and sustained the decision to force the university to admit Hunter and Holmes, state officials closed the university. When it reopened several days later, the two students enrolled and became the first blacks to attend the University of Georgia.

Jordan, then the NAACP field secretary in Georgia, escorted Hunter and Holmes to the registrar's office at the University of Georgia on Monday, January 9, 1961. They worked their way through a crowd of angry, screaming students and refrains of "Two, four, six, eight, we don't want to integrate." The crowd also chanted, "Nigger go home."[88]

Three nights after Hunter and Holmes enrolled and integrated the university, an angry crowd began rioting on the campus. Bricks were thrown through Hunter's dormitory window, and tear gas was used to disperse the mob. Hunter and Holmes were suspended, ostensibly for their own safety, and escorted off the campus by state troopers. They were informed by the dean of students that they were being withdrawn from the university for their own personal safety and for the safety of the other seven thousand students.[89]

Motley filed a petition challenging the suspension. Judge Bootle held a hearing the next day and ordered the university to lift the suspensions and readmit Hunter and Holmes. The two students went back to class under heavy guard on January 16, 1961, but the state continued to appeal the order to admit them.

The case to desegregate the University of Georgia was especially difficult for Motley. The federal district court was in Macon, and the university was in Athens, a hundred miles away. She had to travel to Athens and search through thousands of records to compare the credentials of white applicants who were admitted to those of Hunter and Holmes to prove that they were rejected because of race and not because they were not qualified for admission.

There was no place for Motley to stay overnight in Athens, since the hotels there were racially segregated. As a result, Jordan had to drive her a hundred miles each way every day for several weeks. They had to leave Macon at 6:00 A.M. for a two-hour drive and then drive back another two hours at the end of the day. At lunchtime there was always a problem finding a place to eat because the restaurants and lunch counters in Athens were segregated, too. Looking back on that experience, Motley commented that getting up in order to be on the road by 6:00 A.M., going through records all day, searching for a place to eat lunch, and driving two hundred miles a day was sheer physical exhaustion for her.[90]

Jordan later recalled his own experiences working on the case. "After like a month . . . I was serving subpoenas on the chancellor of the university, the president of the university . . . and the governor. . . . I had not even passed the bar and I'm out serving subpoenas," he said. "The attorney general, Eugene Cook, told me . . . that I would pay a price for that, and I did—I flunked the bar exam! But then, after the lawsuit was filed, we got a subpoena *duces tecum*, which meant that we could go to the university in Athens and go through all of the records.

"I was the youngest lawyer," he continued. "I was the flunky lawyer, I carried the brief cases, I went and got lunches. I did the research. It was my job to pick up Connie Motley at Edmond Thomas's house; he was a lawyer. She had to stay with that family [in Macon] because she couldn't stay anyplace else. It was my job to drive [her] . . . to Athens every day, and we would sit there in the admissions office and go through records after records after records." Jordan was impressed by the kind of intensity Motley exhibited as she looked through the records and searched for evidence to support her case. "She told me what to look for, and after about two weeks I found it," he said.[91]

Motley instructed Jordan on how to review applications and other evidence to prove inequality in the admission process and to prove that the university had discriminated against Hunter and Holmes when it rejected them. It was a relationship with a reversal of gender roles. Jordan, a black man, was taking instruction from and apprenticing under a black woman.

"I found the key piece of evidence that unraveled the University of Georgia's fiction about why the absolutely qualified Charlayne Hunter could not be admitted," he said. The evidence he found demonstrated that after she had been denied admission to the university, a white woman from Marietta, Georgia, with a worse academic record had been admitted. "That made our case. I think we called it prima facie evidence," Jordan said. Motley was pleased that he had found the evidence, and he was pleased, too.

"And then in December was the trial, and I'm still the driver, and Judge Motley sat across from me. I did the driving, and she sat in the other seat and she didn't talk. She didn't look out the window, either," Jordan continued. Motley was completely focused on preparing her questions for the registrar, the chancellor, and the other witnesses as he drove. "She was like a barber who takes his strap, that leather strap—and gets the razor sharp. That's what it reminded me of. . . . Her concentration, her intensity were unbelievable. I mean, if I had to stop the car fast, she just kept reading and kept preparing. Driving for Motley and working as her researcher in the case was the ultimate legal experience. Watching her was a lesson in lawyering itself."[92]

Hunter-Gault, Jordan, and others who were in the courtroom during the trial have described Motley's performance as brilliant. They were especially impressed with her cross-examination of university administrators—It was full of curve balls and ferocious. She was formidable in the courtroom. "She had this way with witnesses of telling [them] to go to hell and making [them] look forward to the trip!" Jordan said.[93]

Motley used the "old clincher" strategy, in which she asked the president, the director of admissions, and the registrar if they would be in favor of accepting a qualified black student into the university. Each of them would have to answer yes.[94]

"The judge was very amused during the whole trial," Motley said. "I guess he was amused by the fact that here I was, a black woman, cross-examining and calling to the stand all of those Georgia officials, who were just squirming, making all kinds of statements that obviously weren't true" about the fact that they didn't have any policy of segregation. "Needless to say, the court was packed with local citizens and other people watching this scene that strengthened the black community. . . . They had not had an opportunity to see this kind of thing, and all of the lawyers on our side were black . . . and of course they had not seen a woman lawyer in most of those parts of the country. Women lawyers were just not in existence. . . . So it was something for the town to turn out for."[95]

During the trial Hunter had to take the witness stand and testify. She later reflected on her experience as a witness and how she tried to emulate Motley's style and performance in the courtroom. "I was a pretty good witness on the stand," she said, "because I had watched Constance Motley in her performance. . . . She was graceful, she was feminine, she was quiet in her interrogation of these people, and she was so calm that they would be lulled into . . . not appreciating that she was about to hit them over the head with the hardest possible question that would reveal their duplicity and lying."[96]

Jordan characterized Motley's victory in the desegregation case against the University of Georgia as "quite significant because it was the first successful desegregation case in higher education in the South and . . . because they [Holmes and Hunter] finished; they graduated and went on to distinguish themselves."[97]

Hunter-Gault was the first black reporter for the *New Yorker*, the second black reporter for the *New York Times*, and the winner of two Emmys. She recently returned to the United States from South Africa, where she was the Johannesburg bureau chief, a foreign correspondent for NPR, and the chief correspondent for CNN. Holmes became a physician.

The noted author Calvin Trillin was the reporter for *Time* magazine and the *New Yorker* during the civil rights movement. While he was covering the South from *Time*'s Atlanta bureau, he went to court every day of the trial and watched Motley desegregate the University of Georgia. He too commented on her expertise in cross-examining hostile witnesses by using the old clincher strategy—that when she asked the admissions director, the registrar, and the president of the university, "Would you be in favor of accepting a qualified Negro into the University of Georgia?", they had to answer yes. The next day, the *Atlanta Journal* noted in a story that "the university registrar has testified in federal court here that he favors admission of qualified Negroes to the university."[98]

Although Trillin spent a great deal of time following and observing Motley in court, she maintained a very disciplined, professional, and distant relationship with him throughout the trial. When asked about his impression of her,

Trillin replied, "She scared the hell out of me. She was a very imposing person . . . she was dead serious, but you also have to realize what sort of situation she was in. . . . She was down there in an atmosphere where it was war, and she was sort of geared up for that, and she wasn't going to be distracted into talking . . . unless she had to."[99]

Motley was extremely focused, intense, confident, and poised in the courtroom throughout the trial. She was also very formal and not self-revelatory. She displayed very little emotion in her interactions with everyone, including Hunter.

Being very formal and dignified was ingrained in Motley. Joel, her son, believes that her formality was effective as a shield and was a natural part of her persona. He attributes it to the influence of her parents, who were from Nevis and were quite formal themselves. "They brought a kind of British slightly distant atmosphere" with them when they immigrated to New Haven, he said.[100]

One day during the trial Motley showed her less formal side and expressed compassion in a private moment with Hunter as they were leaving court. Motley tried to comfort Hunter and let her know that she understood how the ordeal of the trial and being away from her family, school, and social network affected her as a teenager. Motley revealed how the ordeal of the trial was affecting her personally and how she missed her own family, too. Hunter-Gault later described this as the moment that she bonded with Motley and began to feel empowered:

> She [Motley] never paid much attention to me until one day at the end of the week of the trial. . . . I had testified. I wanted to get back to Wayne State University. I had just become a Delta [sorority member]. . . . I wanted to get back to the parties. . . . The lawyers went to the state and asked for permission for me to leave, and they denied it just out of meanness, because they didn't need me as a witness anymore. . . .
>
> So as only a nineteen-year-old could, I sat in the backseat of the car with my lips poked out so far you could just walk on them. I was in a heated funk, and Connie Motley got in the car and sat next to me. And there was a woman who never talked to me, ever, and all of a sudden, she put her hand on my leg and said, "I know how you feel." She said, "I would like to leave this weekend, too. . . . I've been down here a long time. . . . I'd like to be in New York with my husband and twelve-year-old son, whom I haven't seen in a long, long time, but we have a job to do here." And I think from that moment on, there was bonding [between us] beyond her representing me, and that was empowering for me.[101]

Family was very important to Motley. She loved her husband, Joel Wilson Motley Jr.; her son, Joel III; and her extended family. She relished the time she spent with them.

Motley and her husband had a very close and loving relationship and a strong marriage. He was a lawyer, a businessman, and an accomplished professional in his own right. He was also a man who was ahead of his time in his role as a supportive husband. He encouraged Motley to pursue her career as a trial lawyer, played a major role as a caregiver for their son, and assumed other responsibilities in their home that made it possible for his wife to travel extensively and be away from home for extended periods. This enabled her to handle cases for the LDF and still maintain a balance between family life and work.

Joel III commented on the impact his mother's extensive travel and absence from home had on him as a young child and on her relationship with his father. He stated that his mother always made him feel that he was the most important thing in her life, so even though she traveled extensively and was away a great deal of the time, he knew he was loved by her and never felt abandoned.

"My father was a very supportive husband all of the time," he explained, "taking care of me when it was necessary when she was away, but also just encouraging her career. I think he really felt that what she was doing was extremely important, and he wanted to do whatever he could to help her do well at it, which, when you think about the time, was really extraordinary. . . . I don't think there were a lot of men of any ethnic group who could have taken that position as well as my father did."[102] Joel added that his mother and father were happily married for more than fifty years.

In a 1979 *Jet* magazine article, Motley talked about how her marriage and family life remained strong despite the long hours she worked and the extended trips that she took. She gave credit to her husband for being totally involved in what she was doing, sharing the cause she was advocating for, and even traveling to the Supreme Court in Washington to hear her argue civil rights cases when she was an attorney at the LDF.[103]

After successfully forcing the schools in Georgia to desegregate, Motley was called on to help applicants to schools in Mississippi, South Carolina, and other states when they were rejected because of their race. On May 31, 1961, she filed a lawsuit on behalf of James Meredith against the University of Mississippi.

Traditional narratives of the desegregation of the University of Mississippi put the spotlight on Meredith. He was hailed as the brave young man who risked his life and fought to integrate the university. He was even awarded a Congressional Gold Medal.

Although Meredith certainly deserves credit for his valor and perseverance, it is important to point out that he would not have been successful in his quest— and the university would not have been desegregated—without Motley's behind-the-scenes work in the trenches. That work included more than twenty-one trips to the Mississippi district court, more trips to the Fifth Circuit Court of Appeals, and a trip to the Supreme Court to enforce the victory she obtained against the university. She even had to appeal to President Kennedy to send troops to Mississippi to end violent riots in which people were shot and killed.[104] Throughout the ordeal, she spent nights in houses guarded by men with machine guns to protect her from angry segregationists who objected to her advocacy to desegregate the university, and she experienced a great deal of stress, fatigue, harassment, and extended time away from her family to achieve the goal.

Motley filed the desegregation case against the University of Mississippi approximately a year after Meredith had been denied admission and seven years after the *Brown* decision. Emotions in Mississippi were very raw at the time. The racial tensions that lingered after *Brown* escalated when the freedom riders descended on Mississippi at the same time that Motley pursued Meredith's battle to desegregate Ole Miss—the informal name of the all-white university. It was also the term that slaves had used to refer to the wife of the master and plantation owner.

In January 1961 Meredith wrote to the LDF seeking legal assistance in his effort to be admitted to the university. When Thurgood Marshall received the letter, he went into Motley's office, threw the letter on her desk, and said, "This man has got to be crazy." Motley interpreted that as meaning that it would be her case. After she read the letter, Thurgood confirmed her interpretation and said, "That's your case."

Marshall assigned the case to Motley "because she was a woman." His theory was that black women were safer and less subject to violence and attacks in the South than black men because "all white men had black Mammies."[105] Marshall was mistaken. Black women who were civil rights activists were victims of diabolical acts of violence, including vicious beatings, sexual assaults and rape, and even murder in the South.[106]

Marshall left the LDF in 1961 when he was appointed to the Second Circuit Court of Appeals by President Kennedy. After his departure, Motley assumed responsibility for many of his cases and most of the important desegregation cases.[107]

Extreme anger, riots, gunfire, bombs, and death were integral components of the protracted battle to desegregate Ole Miss. They were fueled by the convergence of the Meredith case and the arrival of the freedom riders in Jackson. "White segregationists in Mississippi were enraged" when the freedom riders, determined to break down segregation in transportation, "went and sat in the white waiting rooms at bus and train stations," said Motley.[108] The anger and bitterness from the combination of the two catalytic events caused a combustible reaction, increased the resistance to desegregation, and resulted in mob violence and death.

Neither Motley nor any of the other LDF attorneys had anticipated the freedom riders. She commented on them as follows: "Finally we [the LDF] decided to bring this suit, and we got it ready, and lo and behold . . . at that very time . . . the freedom riders arrived in Jackson. I remember going into court in Jackson . . . before Judge Mize. [He] just shook his head and said, 'Why did you have to come now? He knew that we had a situation which had literally inflamed the state, and we were going to have the same kind of trouble we had with the Autherine Lucy case in Alabama. And of course, sure enough, we did."[109]

James Meredith was born and raised in Mississippi. He received an honorable discharge from the air force after serving in Japan. Upon his return to Mississippi in 1960, he attended Jackson State College, an all-black institution. In January 1961 he requested admission to the University of Mississippi as a transfer student. The application required references from six alumni and a photograph. He did not know six alumni of the all-white university that had never had a black graduate, so he attached recommendations from six blacks along with a photograph of himself and submitted his application.

He was rejected twice. The first rejection letter stated that the university was overcrowded and could not admit more applicants that semester; however, hundreds of white students were subsequently admitted. Meredith reapplied the next semester and received a second rejection letter; it informed him that the university had a new rule that it accepted only students from accredited institutions, and Jackson State was not accredited. When he received the second rejection, Meredith wrote to the LDF and asked for assistance.[110]

The case was assigned to Motley, and that began the prolonged and bitter legal and political battle against the University of Mississippi and Governor Ross Barnett to get Meredith admitted and registered. Intervention was required by President Kennedy and his brother, US Attorney General Robert Kennedy, to end the deadly violence, but Motley was finally victorious.

When Motley filed the lawsuit against the university on May 31, 1961, she sought a preliminary injunction to allow Meredith to register for classes in the summer session scheduled to begin on June 8, 1961.[111] She needed a lawyer admitted to practice in Mississippi to serve as local counsel in the case, and there were only three black lawyers in Mississippi at the time. One of them, R. Jess Brown, agreed to accept service of papers and cooperate with Motley as local counsel in the case. He also worked as a cooperating lawyer with the LDF in the freedom rider cases.

Judge Sidney C. Mize set the hearing for June 12, 1961. Motley traveled from New York to Mississippi for the hearing on June 12; however, Judge Mize suspended the proceedings and reset the hearing for July 10. Motley returned to Mississippi on July 10 only to discover that the hearing would be reset again. The hearing finally began on August 10 and was held over three days: August 10,

15, and 16. Judge Mize did not issue his ruling in *Meredith v. Fair* until December 1, 1961, and he held that Meredith had not been denied admission because of his race. Motley appealed the ruling to the Fifth Circuit Court of Appeals.[112]

The fight Motley waged to desegregate Ole Miss, often referred to as "the Last Battle of the Civil War," lasted more than eighteen months. She had to make constant trips from New York to Mississippi and appeal all the way up to the Supreme Court. Although Motley finally won the case in court, she still had to elicit the support of President Kennedy and federal troops to implement the victory over the university.[113]

After four unsuccessful attempts to enroll in the university, Meredith finally succeeded on October 1, 1962. Federal marshals accompanied him when he went to register on September 30. Although he was escorted by the marshals at night under cover of darkness, word quickly spread that he was on the campus. By 7:00 P.M. a large group of angry students and racist citizens from rural areas in Mississippi had assembled in Oxford and around Ole Miss. The mob threw bricks and lead pipes; they ignited bottles filled with gasoline (Molotov cocktails) and threw them, too. They burned automobiles in the parking lots, and they viciously attacked newspaper and television reporters and cameramen who were covering the story. Tear gas canisters exploded, and gunfire erupted. The out-of-control mob also used bulldozers, fire engines, and cars to attack the US marshals. Two or three people were killed, and hundreds were hurt. The body of a French journalist, Paul Guihard, was found with a bullet in the back. The body of a local jukebox repairman was found with a bullet in his head. In addition, 166 marshals (4 of them shot), and 48 soldiers were injured.[114]

Around midnight, after five hours of rioting, President Kennedy was forced to federalize members of the Mississippi National Guard and send five thousand federal troops and four hundred deputy US marshals to Oxford. He sent them to end the riots and restore law and order on the Ole Miss campus and in the city of Oxford, *not* to enforce court-ordered desegregation. He also federalized other regular infantrymen, prison guards, border patrols, and military police across the state line in Tennessee and sent them, too.[115]

It took more than eight hours to subdue the rioters. The violence on the campus and in Oxford did not end until 8:00 A.M. on October 1, thirteen hours after it had erupted and after more than three hundred rioters had been taken into custody.

This case marked the second time a US president was forced to use federal troops in a school desegregation case. The first, as we have already seen, was when President Eisenhower reluctantly sent troops to Central High School in Little Rock, Arkansas, to safely escort nine black students into the school.

Jack Greenberg described Motley as indomitable in the *Meredith* case. "She would take on a project like opening up the University of Mississippi and just keep coming back again and again. . . . She just dug in there and stayed there until they rolled over," he said. Elaborating further, he stated, "When she'd go after some of those Southern defendants, it was like [Ulysses] Grant at Vicksburg. She would dig in, appealing in case after case until she defeated them." He, too, analogized Motley's relentless effort to force the University to admit Meredith to "the Last Battle of the Civil War."[116]

Derrick Bell affirmed Greenberg's characterization of Motley's tenacity in the ordeal to desegregate the University of Mississippi. "The *Meredith* case was a remarkable exhibition of her talents, which were persistence, never say die," he recalled. "She had to deal with James Meredith, who could be very difficult, and she also had to deal with segregationist judges who were disrespectful to her."[117] During the trials at each level of the case, some segregationist judges turned their backs to Motley and faced the wall when she got up to make an argument. They openly displayed their disrespect for her and their readiness to rule against her before she even began her presentation. Bell was extremely impressed by the way Motley dealt with Meredith and the segregationist judges and how she kept her focus and won the case.

After more than eighteen months and twenty-one trips to the trial court in Mississippi, the court of appeals, and the Supreme Court to litigate in what was characterized as the eerie atmosphere of never-never land, Motley finally succeeded in getting Meredith enrolled in Ole Miss. At that point all the dangerous and hard work had been done. That's when the US Justice Department tried to intervene and take over the *Meredith* case.

Motley rejected the overture from the Justice Department. She was angered by its presumptuousness in thinking that it could take over her case. She was especially upset because it had not offered any assistance or protection up to that point. Motley openly expressed her anger and slammed the phone on Attorney General Kennedy's aide when the message was conveyed that the Justice Department wanted to take over. She emphatically stated that the department could join her if it liked, but she was moving forward as the lead lawyer in the case.[118]

Once Meredith was enrolled in Ole Miss and began to attend, US deputy marshals and army troops guarded him twenty-four hours a day until he graduated with a degree in political science on August 18, 1963.[119]

The state of Mississippi retaliated against Motley for her victory in forcing the desegregation of Ole Miss. It resorted to intimidation tactics and sued her for something nonsensical like failure to pay a tax as an outside lawyer coming into the state, she said.[120]

Motley commented on the persistent racism and acts of violence in Mississippi as well as in Alabama and Arkansas in her work to implement the desegregation order in *Brown*. Although the LDF and the NAACP as a whole had anticipated resistance to the implementation of *Brown* and opposition to the end of segregation, "they had not foreseen the extent of mob violence and the necessity for federal troops to be utilized on more than one occasion to put down official resistance to the decision." Motley noted. The "first thing . . . civil rights lawyers learned about mob resistance to desegregation was that President Eisenhower was unenthusiastic about enforcing the *Brown* decision, particularly if it meant the mobilization of a state's national guard or sending in federal troops or marshals from outside the state" to facilitate desegregation of schools. Motley believed that if Eisenhower had "made a strong statement endorsing the Supreme Court's decision" in *Brown* or had declared his duty as president to enforce the decision, "the whole course of massive resistance might have been different."[121]

Motley criticized the federal government's failure to provide protection for Autherine Lucy at the University of Alabama. The "uncivilized mob response" in the *Lucy* case "was against the backdrop of the wholly spontaneous Montgomery Bus Boycott" led by Jo Ann Robinson. She also criticized Eisenhower for failing to leave his golf game in Rhode Island to address the crisis in Arkansas during the desegregation of Central High. She commented on the lack of experience that "President Kennedy and his attorney general brother" had dealing with segregationist elected officials in the South and the manner in which the governor of Mississippi manipulated them and failed to provide state troopers to protect Meredith when he initially attempted to enter the Ole Miss campus to enroll.[122]

Meredith was personally exposed to great danger in Mississippi, and Motley was, too. Although she did not frighten easily, Motley actually feared for her life, especially in Clarksdale, where she had to visit an NAACP chapter. She was patently aware that anything could happen there. The state had a well-documented history of violence against blacks, and many of the rural whites there vehemently opposed desegregation. They embraced a system that explicitly confined blacks to a subjugated situation.[123]

Mississippi was the worst state Motley worked in. The "fear of violence was greater there . . . than any other place," she recalled, "and there was less protection" there because "fewer people in the black community were willing to be identified with the NAACP . . . they really feared economic and physical reprisals."[124] Blacks who engaged in or were simply "suspected of engaging in NAACP activities [in Mississippi] faced reprisals, which included the calling in or refusal of loans, eviction, closure of credit, exorbitant utility rates, and even the disconnecting of utilities."[125] They also faced physical reprisals that included beatings and even lynching. As a result, most blacks "were intimidated to the point where they didn't even join the NAACP, and if anybody asked if they were members of the NAACP, they would say, 'Of course not.'" Many black people in Mississippi were even "afraid to be seen at an NAACP meeting."[126] Motley understood their reluctance and fear because she too had experiences that caused her to be very afraid for her safety while in the state.

"I remember being in Clarksdale and being very fearful because it was so rural and blacks seemed so deprived there, and the general atmosphere was kind of eerie," she said. "There were, as far as you could see, nothing but cotton fields and a cotton mill whining all night long. It was so desolate—the abandoned shacks where blacks once lived . . . and worked the cotton fields . . . were being worked by machines when I was there. I remember being anxious to get out of there, because it seemed like a community where anything could happen and absolutely nothing would be done. And, of course . . . later those three young boys [civil rights activists James Chaney, Michael Schwerner, and Andrew Goodman]. . . were murdered and buried in an earthen dam there" in 1963 and their bodies were not found for quite a long time.[127]

The violence Motley spoke about in Mississippi was documented at length by Francoise Hamlin. She described the rape, murder, unprovoked assaults, vicious beatings, lynchings, and other forms of brutal murder of blacks in Mississippi and the bombing of their homes. She found that all too often, Southern "justice" meant that the white perpetrators of violent acts against blacks walked away with no legal consequences for their actions.[128]

Although hotels in Mississippi were segregated and most local blacks were afraid to have Motley stay in their homes, Medgar Evers, the NAACP secretary for the state of Mississippi, did open his home to her. Less than six months after Evers was appointed to his position, his name was at the top of "the death list circulating among the state's extremist groups." Evers soon realized that he was "a marked man" because of his visible position in the NAACP. He realized that black people in Mississippi were afraid to associate with him. They "shunned him, hoping to avoid potential stray bullets" intended for him.[129]

Evers always met Motley at the airport when she arrived in Mississippi. In fact, he was the person who first notified her that James Meredith had applied for admission to the University of Mississippi. While she was working on the *Meredith* case, Evers drove Motley to Meridian, Mississippi, where Judge Mize was sitting, so that she could argue the case. She described the fear she experienced one night while they were traveling to Meridian and Evers said to her, "Don't look back now, but we're being followed." He made the comment as they "came to a stretch of road where there were no houses" and while she "was busy writing out something in longhand." It was a terrifying experience. When they got to Meridian, "Medgar was able to see that it was the state police" following his car. "They knew Medgar's car; they knew the license number," and they had him under constant surveillance because of his association with the NAACP, Motley said.[130] They followed him all the time. The state police were sometimes prone to commit violence against blacks involved in the civil rights movement.

Motley stayed over in Meridian that night, but it was yet another time that she stayed awake all night. She could not sleep because she had no protection. There were no men with guns guarding the house that night.

In addition to her victories in the cases to desegregate the University of Alabama, the University of Georgia, and the University of Mississippi, Motley was the LDF lawyer who won the case to desegregate Clemson College in South Carolina after Harvey Gantt had been rejected for admission to the School of Engineering. Because of her efforts, Gantt was the first black student to enroll and complete his graduate education at what later became Clemson University. Motley also won the case to desegregate Louisiana State University; she represented Ernest Morial who became the first black student admitted to the law school. He subsequently became the mayor of New Orleans.

In 1962, almost a full decade after the Supreme Court's *Brown* ruling, public schools in Savannah, Georgia, were still racially segregated. The NAACP filed a lawsuit in the federal district court in Savannah to desegregate the public school system in Chatham County.

Frank M. Scarlett, a judge who personally opposed desegregation and disapproved of the decision in *Brown*, heard the case and issued a ruling in *Stell v. Savannah-Chatham County Bd. of Ed*. He held that desegregation would psychologically harm both black children and white children and ruled that segregation was therefore still constitutionally permissible in Savannah despite the Supreme Court's ruling in *Brown*.[131] Motley appealed his ruling to the Fifth Circuit Court of Appeals. Again she was victorious—Judge Elbert Tuttle overruled Scarlett and entered an order to desegregate the schools in Savannah.[132]

Motley was also an attorney in the case to desegregate schools in New Orleans. Beginning in early 1960 until the end of the year, she was accompanied by Jack Greenberg and Jim Nabritt, two other LDF lawyers, in her constant commutation from New York to Louisiana state and district courts and the court of appeals, where she was always greeted by picketers and angry white protesters who shouted insults and shoved her. She was not fazed by their antics, however. Instead, Motley and the other attorneys ignored them, persevered, and performed work in the courts that resulted in the desegregation of schools.

Victory was achieved on November 13, 1960, when Judge Skelly Wright issued an order compelling the admission of four little black girls to public schools in New Orleans. He also issued a restraining order prohibiting the Louisiana State Legislature, the governor, and all others from interfering with the operation of Orleans Parish schools.[133]

On November 14 the four girls (Ruby Bridges, Gaile Etienne, Tessie Prevost, and Leonia Tate) entered the formerly all-white schools. They were escorted by federal marshals, who led them through the gauntlet of angry whites. As the children walked past them, the mob jeered, shouted insults, and sang "Glory, glory segregation" to the tune of "The Battle Hymn of the Republic." Two days after they desegregated the schools, violence erupted in New Orleans. It began when a group of whites demonstrated against school integration, assaulted blacks, and committed acts of vandalism. Some blacks retaliated and threw rocks. White parents in Louisiana boycotted the schools for a while, keeping their children at home rather than sending them to schools with black students.

Motley was often thrust into situations where things were always changing— and changing very fast, in her desegregation cases. A multitude of things happened that she had not and could not have anticipated. Her experience in New Orleans provides an example of how rapidly things changed and how her work became much more difficult.

In New Orleans she quickly realized that in addition to challenging actions by segregationist governors and school administrators who physically blocked black students from entering schools, she also had to deal with hostile state legislatures that enacted laws nullifying *Brown* and declaring that the Supreme Court's ruling did not have any effect in their states. While Motley was litigating the case to desegregate the public schools in New Orleans, the legislature immediately enacted a "whole raft of laws obviously unconstitutional" to avoid desegregation. Although the laws were unconstitutional, she still had to challenge them. She had "to go to court and get every one of them knocked out."[134]

Motley also unexpectedly found herself going to courts in other states where segregationist legislatures had quickly adopted laws to prevent the desegregation of their schools. She had to argue the school desegregation cases as well as challenge all of the newly enacted laws. She often had to prepare for emergency hearings because the laws were adopted right before the beginning of the academic year, and they had to be invalidated in order for black students to enroll and attend classes that year.

On many occasions Motley had to argue her cases in front of judges who were personally opposed to desegregation, who were hostile to blacks, and who refused to enforce the decision in *Brown*.[135] Although they had an obligation to uphold the law, the segregationist judges abused their power and used tactics in their courts that contributed to making Motley's experience unpleasant, extremely difficult, and sometimes dangerous. Some judges openly demonstrated their disdain for her because of her advocacy to end segregation.[136]

In many communities the resistance to the implementation of *Brown* was actively aided by the segregationist judges. This was particularly true in Mississippi, Florida, Louisiana, Alabama, Georgia, and Tennessee, where some state and federal court judges strenuously resisted desegregation. All this resistance required Motley to spend more time confronting angry racist crowds as she tried to enter and exit courts. It also required her to appeal decisions rendered by the hostile judges.[137]

Motley's unpleasant experience with Judge William Harrold Cox in Meridian, Mississippi, provides an example of an extremely hostile federal judge whose action forced Motley to file multiple appeals. He refused to give up even after she had gone all the way to the Supreme Court and obtained a ruling compelling him to order James Meredith's admission to Ole Miss.

Motley's secretary, Roberta Thomas, had made a "typographical error in a hastily prepared" motion to hold the university officials in contempt and to enjoin the governor from blocking Meredith's entrance to the university after she had won the case against it. Thomas had inadvertently typed the word *Order* instead of *Motion* on the document. When Motley attempted to hand it to Judge Mize, who was also sitting on the case, Judge Cox snatched it from her. He saw the error and angrily threw the paper across the table at her.[138] At that point Mize reminded Cox that "the case had been fought all the way through the courts, it had been up to the Supreme Court and they had lost, and they had done all that they could in Mississippi to resist this [desegregation], and having lost, it was time to comply with the law" and grant the order to compel the governor to allow Meredith to enroll at the university.[139]

Motley was "amazed that the man [Cox] would demonstrate such lack of judicial temperament in front of lawyers, particularly one from the Justice Department" who was in the courtroom. She was especially amazed that during his display of anger and poor judicial conduct, Cox accused the Justice Department lawyer, a white male, "of being a nigger lover . . . because he just despised blacks so" and "he despised any whites who would pursue in his court black rights."[140] In her autobiography, Motley wrote that "Judge Cox proved to be the most openly racist judge ever to sit on a federal court bench in this country."[141]

In Dallas Motley encountered another segregationist judge. He simply "rendered a decision saying that he disagreed with the Supreme Court decision" in *Brown* and wasn't going to do anything to facilitate desegregation in Texas.[142]

Florida was one of the states where Motley often appeared before segregationist judges. As the attorney in twelve elementary school desegregation cases in that state, she filed lawsuits in Pensacola, Jacksonville, Palm Beach, and Tampa.

Many of the judges in Florida were not only hostile to the idea of desegregation, they also abused their power and tried to control, if not prevent, integration of the state's schools. For example, the case to desegregate the University of Florida in Gainesville remained pending in the state courts for nine years because the judge would not hear it. A petition finally had to be filed with the Supreme Court to compel the judge to hear the case.[143]

In Tampa Motley encountered another judge who was hostile and unalterably opposed to desegregation. His resistance was so great that he just refused to hear the case. "We filed a case involving the Tampa school system," Motley explained, "and Judge Whitehurst, an elderly man, was a segregationist, and he would not even permit the case to be argued" in his court.[144] Although the case was on his docket, the judge wouldn't call it, so she could not argue it, and there was no way to go over his head. The judge finally stepped down, and this was the only way that Motley and the LDF finally got the case called up for trial.[145]

Segregationist judges refused to enforce the decision in *Brown* because they were part of the whole deeply rooted system of segregation that Motley, the LDF, and the NAACP were attacking. The judges had grown up in that system, and they embraced it. They saw integration as a threat to the social structure and way of life in the South. "To them," Motley noted, "it did not involve simply the admission of one black to a classroom. If that were the beginning and the end of it, there would not have been so much resistance. . . . They knew that essentially what was involved was an attack on the social structure of the South that dictated segregation of blacks and their exclusion from institutions" and society at large. Blacks were just not part of the body politic in the South. "Segregation was the way of life, . . . and these judges, having grown up in that system, having developed it, being a part of it, obviously presented the same kind of resistance you'd get from anyone whose entire life style was being threatened," Motley added.[146]

The segregationist judges knew that like Marshall, Motley wasn't just arguing to desegregate a particular school or university in their courtrooms. They knew that the LDF attorneys were really arguing for the end of segregation and the entire way of life in the South that segregationists knew and supported.

John R. Lewis—the US Representative for the Fifth Congressional District in Georgia; a former civil rights leader who participated in sit-ins, freedom rides, marches, and mass demonstrations; and a former chairman of SNCC—eloquently summarized the position of both the segregationists and the civil rights activists during the movement. He stated that when LDF attorneys Motley and Marshall came to town, everybody "knew there would be a shake-up for the cause of justice."[147]

Figure 1. Constance Baker Motley upon her graduation from New York University, 1943. Courtesy of Joel Motley III.

Figure 2. Clarence Blakeslee, from "History of Class of 1885, Sheffield Scientific School," vol. 3, page 23. Yale University Manuscripts and Archives, image no. 865.

Figure 3. Wedding of Constance Baker and Joel Wilson Motley Jr., St. Luke's Episcopal Church, New Haven, Connecticut, August 18, 1946. Courtesy of Joel Motley III.

Figure 4. Constance Baker Motley and Thurgood Marshall, ca.1960.

Figure 5. NAACP Legal Defense and Education Fund staff with Constance Baker Motley, working on the James Meredith case.

Figure 6. Constance Baker Motley with boxes of letters received from people all over the world during the James Meredith case, 1962.

Figure 7. Coretta Scott King, Martin Luther King Jr., and Constance Baker Motley, honoring Rosa Parks at the Southern Christian Leadership Conference, 1965. Courtesy of the SCLC.

Figure 8. Constance Baker Motley and President Lyndon Johnson in the Oval Office on the day he nominated her to a federal judgeship, January 25, 1966. Courtesy of the Library of Congress.

Figure 9. Constance Baker Motley in her judicial robe. Courtesy of the Federal District Court Southern District of New York.

Figure 10. Constance Baker Motley with her client Harvey Gantt (left) and fellow attorney W. T. Smith (right), 1962. Courtesy of the Library of Congress.

Figure 11. Constance Baker Motley at a City Hall budget meeting, 1965. Courtesy of the Library of Congress.

Figure 12. Constance Baker Motley being sworn in by Mayor Robert F. Wagner at City Hall as the new borough president of Manhattan, 1965. Courtesy of the Library of Congress.

Figure 13. Constance Baker Motley signing papers as the new "lady borough president," 1965. Courtesy of the Library of Congress.

Figure 14. Charles J. Ogletree, Ernest Green, Bernard Lafayette, Drew S. Days III, and Derrick Bell, Life of Judge Constance Baker Motley Symposium, 2009. From the private collection of Gary Ford.

Figure 15. Joel Wilson Motley III, the son of Constance Baker Motley, and her niece, Constance Royster, 2009. From the private collection of Gary Ford.

5

Representing Protesters

Mass Demonstrations, Marches,
Sit-Ins, and Freedom Rides

In the heart of the American South, during the early days of the civil rights
movement in the late '50s and [the] '60s, there were only two lawyers that
made white segregationists tremble and gave civil rights workers hope:
Constance Baker Motley and Thurgood Marshall. When someone mentioned that one of them was coming to town, we knew there would be a
shake-up for the cause of justice.
——Congressman John Lewis to the US House of Representatives,
December 2, 2005

In addition to her school desegregation work, Constance Baker Motley was an attorney in *Rice v. Elmore*, a voting rights case in South Carolina, where blacks had
been excluded from voting in Democratic Party primary elections.[1] The LDF took
the case because the exclusion constituted a violation of the Fifteenth Amendment and because primary elections are an integral part of the election process.[2]
The case was important in protecting the rights of blacks to register and to vote.
It was important to gain access for blacks to the political power structure; to em-
power them to become politically active; to force elected officials on the local,
state, and national level to represent their interests; and to facilitate the development of black political power.

Motley sued and won public accommodation cases when blacks were excluded from state parks in South Carolina and Tennessee because of their race.
She also represented Dr. Martin Luther King Jr. and other activists who participated in protest marches, boycotts, sit-ins, and freedom rides across the country
and forced their release when they were arrested and locked up in Southern jails.

Reverend Wyatt Tee Walker, King's chief of staff and the former executive director of the SCLC, was one of the protesters jailed during the civil rights movement. He reminisced about Motley's representation of him as follows:

First and foremost, Constance Baker Motley was the quintessential
lady, a worthy role model for any young woman of African descent or any

descent. An able and highly qualified practitioner of American jurisprudence. I am not sure how many times she represented me personally, but she was perennially in court for participants of the Movement. She conducted herself with great aplomb in spite of being confronted in southern courts with all kinds of discourtesies that would not be allowed in American courts elsewhere. I do know she represented my wife and me in Mississippi very ably.

Judge Motley was always the epitome of grace and regal bearing. I remember her as being eloquent and speaking with the assurance that is usually coupled with high intellect. Her pronouncements in court were never bombastic or tinged with bitterness or satire. Even her tone of voice was measured, and I'm sure the defense counsel was awed by her knowledge of the law despite the fact that she represented the "enemy." It was obvious the judges felt they were being lectured to by a person far above them in academic preparation and personal talent. There was no way to camouflage her immense talents.[3]

Motley also represented King, Reverend Ralph Abernathy (the cofounder of the SCLC and an executive board member), and other SCLC members when they were arrested and jailed during what has been characterized as the stormy protest days in the South.[4] Reverend Andrew Young often joined in those battles. He too was arrested during those stormy days.

King referred to those days in a Western Union telegram he sent to Motley on February 10, 1964. "We have been in many battles together," he wrote. Motley replied, "We have indeed been in many battles together and will be in the future."[5]

Motley regularly went to the South to represent King and the protesters who participated in mass demonstrations with him. "King constantly consulted with us about what he was lawfully permitted to do" in connection with marches and other forms of protest, she said, "and whether certain programs . . . would run into difficulty, such as boycotts of businesses and . . . whether they were required to get certain kinds of permits or whether they were permitted to sit in in a capitol or state office building itself or whether they were limited to the sidewalk. . . . He would seek to get advice on how far the demonstrators could go and that kind of thing."[6]

Andrew Young added, "Martin never sought advice on whether he should move forward with action he planned to take, even if he knew he would be arrested and put in jail. And Motley was not the type of attorney who would advise him not to go forward with the protest or other action such as a march without obtaining the legally required permit. . . . She would simply tell him, 'I'll do my best to get you all out of jail.'"[7] Sometimes, noted Bernard Lafayette, getting them out of jail required "Sidney Poitier and Harry Belafonte to drive all night long with thousands of dollars" in suitcases to pay protesters' fines and cover other expenses required to keep the SCLC offices open. Aretha Franklin, Sammy Davis Jr., and other performers provided money for the movement, too.[8]

As a result of the constant involvement with King, Motley developed a very close relationship with him and was frequently called upon to represent him and those who were arrested with him. She represented King in Albany when an injunction was issued against him and the march he planned to lead. She also represented him in Birmingham, Atlanta, and other places when he was arrested and jailed.[9]

Historians wrote extensively about events of national significance, including marches and mass protests led by King; however, they failed to examine in depth the importance of Motley's out-of-the-spotlight action and agency, which included constantly flying to Georgia, Alabama, and other places in the South to secure King's release from jail, to remove injunctions against marches, and to make it possible for him to lead the large protests that the media highlighted. Without Motley's behind-the-scenes courtroom work, many of the marches and other forms of protest might not have occurred.

For example, historians focused on King's campaign in Albany and how the successful campaign in Birmingham brought much-needed support from people who had previously not supported him or the movement. What they did not focus on, however, was the fact that if Motley had not prevailed in court, the march King led in Albany might not have taken place at all. And if she had not engaged in exhaustive litigation in both the trial court in Birmingham and the appellate court in Atlanta (in a single day) and obtained an order to reinstate students who had been expelled for participating in the march with King, the Birmingham campaign might have been a failure, and support for him and the civil rights movement might have been lost.

Helping blacks attain all the attributes of first-class citizenship by nonviolent direct action was the goal of the SCLC. The right to vote was one of the most important attributes. King and the SCLC recognized that it was necessary to increase the extraordinarily small number of blacks who voted; they wanted "every Negro in the South to register and to vote."[10] To achieve the goal, they initiated the Crusade for Citizenship campaign to register two million black voters in the South and to double the number who voted by the 1958 and 1960 elections.[11]

The Crusade for Citizenship did not achieve its goal of registering a large number of black voters, and it was deemed by some to be a failure; however, King and the SCLC were not deterred. They continued to organize campaigns and work with other civil rights groups to end racial discrimination and help blacks attain equal rights in the South and throughout the country.

In 1961 black organizations gathered in Albany, Georgia, to conduct a broad campaign, known as the Albany Movement, to challenge institutionalized racial segregation and discrimination in all aspects in that city. In mid-November Albany State College students and other activists began to be arrested and jailed when they attempted to use the all-white facilities in the Albany bus terminal to test compliance with the Interstate Commerce Commission (ICC) ruling, which had become effective on November 1, that banned segregation in interstate bus facilities.[12]

The demonstrations escalated after Thanksgiving Day and continued into the Christmas season. Hundreds of students and other activists—including Albany State College students who defied their dean's directions to use "colored-only" facilities—staged sit-ins, marches, and boycotts. Many of the protesters were viciously beaten, arrested, and jailed, and students were also expelled.[13]

With hundreds of protesters in jail and no funds to secure their release, the Albany Movement began to lose its momentum. The leaders reached out to King and the SCLC for support. They asked King to come to Albany to reenergize the movement and to be the catalyst for national media coverage of it, and he acquiesced to their request. He and Abernathy went to Albany, made speeches, held mass meetings, led marches on city hall, and were arrested and jailed. King was transferred to Sumter County Jail in Americus, Georgia.[14]

Some protesters refused bail, choosing instead to remain in jail to highlight the plight of blacks in Albany. King also refused bail; he declared that he would remain in jail through the 1961 Christmas season to protest segregation and racial discrimination.[15] His incarceration brought the Albany Movement national media coverage.

City officials developed a strategy to get King out of Albany so they could end the negative spotlight on their city. They made an agreement with the leaders of the Albany Movement, promising that they would comply with the ICC ruling to desegregate the bus terminals and would release the jailed protesters if King would leave the city immediately. King was convinced that the movement had achieved its goal and that the city officials would honor their agreement, so he left Albany as soon as he was released. The city officials, however, failed to honor their agreement.[16] Institutionalized segregation continued to be the official policy in the city, and the protest demonstrations and arrest of blacks continued into August 1962.

King returned to Albany with members of the SCLC staff and coordinated a campaign to combat the policy and practice of segregation. He organized protesters and led a major march. This time King and the SCLC were outwitted by Laurie Pritchett, the Albany police chief, who directed his officers to refrain from any form of violence or brutality that could be captured by television cameras or newspaper reporters when they arrested King and the protesters and took them to jail. Pritchett filled not only the jails in Albany but also jails in surrounding communities.[17] After most of the protesters were jailed, the movement lost momentum; the media and some historians portrayed King and the SCLC as having been defeated in Albany.

Motley first became personally acquainted with King when she was sent by the LDF to represent him in Albany early in 1962. On a Friday afternoon a judge issued an injunction against a protest march that King planned to lead with the Albany Movement on Sunday.[18] After he issued the injunction, the "judge rushed out of town" and went to Florida for the weekend so that King would not be able to satisfy the two days' notice requirement to have city officials vacate the injunction and lift the restriction on the march.[19]

Donald Hollowell, the local counsel for the LDF in Atlanta, called Motley and asked her to "come down and help us because we want to get this injunction lifted" so the march can take place.[20] She got on a plane Sunday evening, arrived in Albany around midnight, and went to court the next day to argue for the removal of the injunction. She prevailed in court, and as a result King was able to lead the march. Hollowell worked with Motley on the case.

Upon her arrival in Albany, Motley encountered William Kunstler, a white male attorney, who had accompanied Hollowell and C. B. King, the local attorney for the protesters, to the airport to pick her up. Although Motley barely knew Kunstler, he pushed ahead of Hollowell and King and kissed and embraced her like a long-lost friend.[21] He told her that he was Martin Luther King's lawyer and suggested that they should divide the argument in court, with him making the opening statement and laying out the facts of the case for the judge and Motley following him with the substantive argument on the law and the rebuttal.[22] Motley had not spoken with Dr. King in person before her arrival in Albany; therefore, she assumed what Kunstler told her about being King's personal lawyer was true.[23]

Motley stayed up all night preparing her papers and argument for the appeal of the injunction against the march. The next morning she and Kunstler went to the Fifth Circuit Court of Appeals. When they got inside the courtroom, Motley said, Kunstler took over. He "jumped up to address the court before anyone else could" and said, "Judge Tuttle . . . I would like to introduce Mrs. Motley from New York" to the court.[24] The judge responded, "Mr. Kunstler, Mrs. Motley has appeared here so often I sometimes think she's a member of this court. We'll hear the jurisdictional question first." Kunstler replied, "Oh, Mrs. Motley will argue that." Motley argued the case with Martin Luther King sitting in the courtroom. As she and Kunstler turned around to leave the courtroom, King and his wife, Coretta, were sitting on the first bench. They greeted Motley, but "King did not greet Kunstler or introduce him as his lawyer."[25]

Motley's representation of King in Albany was followed by continual court appearances on his behalf. She represented him many more times, including in

Selma and Birmingham, where he was arrested and jailed regularly.[26] Sometimes King was physically assaulted by the police when he was arrested, but he was never assaulted in public.[27]

Martin Luther King and the SCLC reflected on and learned from their experience in Albany, and they used it to develop their strategy for future campaigns, including the very successful Birmingham campaign. In 1963 the SCLC, together with the Alabama Christian Movement for Human Rights, launched a campaign to attack institutionalized segregation in Birmingham by engaging in sit-ins and demanding service at all-white facilities, marching on city hall and the registrar of voters county building, and holding mass meetings, kneel-ins at churches, and boycotts of white merchants in downtown Birmingham. The goal of the campaign was to desegregate all public places, to obtain equal employment opportunities for blacks, and to free protesters who had been arrested and jailed in prior demonstrations.

The SCLC organized protesters to picket all establishments that discriminated against blacks. Many of the protesters were arrested and charged with breach of the peace, trespassing, loitering, and participating in parades without permits in violation of a local city ordinance. Of course, no permits would have been granted for the protests even if they had been requested.

Just before Easter in 1963, King announced that he would lead demonstrations and boycotts of downtown stores in Birmingham to protest the legally enforced policies and practices of racial segregation and of discrimination in employment. The campaign was launched during the Easter shopping season in order to inflict the greatest economic pain and disruption on the city through nonviolent protest.[28]

Immediately after King's announcement, the Birmingham city attorney went to court and sought a temporary restraining order to prevent the marches that were scheduled to take place on Good Friday and Easter Sunday. The restraining order, which prohibited the marches without a permit, was served on King at the Gaston Motel on April 11. Motley and the LDF staff, along with King, Abernathy, Young, and other SCLC staffers, often used the Gaston Motel as their base of operations in Birmingham. After he was served, King issued a press release in which he stated that in good conscience he could not obey the injunction and that his action in moving forward with the nonviolent protest marches would not be out of disrespect for the law but out of the highest respect for it.[29]

King proceeded to lead the march on Good Friday, April 12, 1963, with Abernathy by his side. They were arrested, convicted of contempt, sentenced to five days in jail, and each placed in solitary confinement. While he was jailed, King wrote his historic "Letter from Birmingham City Jail" on the margins of the

Birmingham News. The letter was written in response to a statement published in that paper by eight clergymen in Birmingham who criticized King and the protest action.[30]

The SCLC had acquiesced to the urging of James Bevel, an SCLC organizer, and used elementary and high school students in the marches in Birmingham.[31] Thousand of protesters, including these students, were arrested and jailed. Unlike Laurie Pritchett in Albany, Birmingham Police Chief Eugene "Bull" Connor ordered his police to use tear gas, fire hoses, and police dogs to disperse the protesters. "Reporters from around the world had poured into Birmingham to cover the events."[32] The media captured live footage of the children and other protesters being gassed, beaten by club-swinging policemen, attacked by vicious police dogs, and assaulted with high-pressure fire department water hoses. That horrific scene of excessive force used on peaceful protesters was broadcast on television and appeared in newspapers around the world.

The media's exposure of the brutality and violence leashed on the nonviolent demonstration had a direct beneficial effect; in fact, it was pivotal. It publicized the oppression and violence black people encountered in their struggle to end racial segregation and obtain basic human rights in the United States. It triggered international outrage and brought much-needed sympathy and support from many people on the local, regional, and national levels who had not previously supported the civil rights movement

Despite criticism from the clergy, business leaders, and others, the Birmingham campaign was successful; the SCLC achieved a major victory over Jim Crow through nonviolent direct action. On May 10, 1963, King announced an agreement in which the city officials agreed to remove all white-only and black-only signs from restrooms and drinking fountains, to implement a plan to desegregate lunch counters and other facilities, to provide employment opportunities for blacks, and to release jailed protesters.[33]

The ugly face of segregation appeared in the aftermath of King's announcement. Angered by the agreement, white segregationists in Birmingham bombed the Gaston Motel, the SCLC headquarters in Birmingham. They also bombed the home of King's brother, Alfred Daniel King. And in an outrageous act of brutality, four young black girls—Addie Mae Collins, Cynthia Wesley, Carole Robertson, and Carol Denise McNair—were killed when members of the Ku Klux Klan bombed the Sixteenth Street Baptist Church on September 15, 1963.

The Birmingham campaign was one of the most significant events of the civil rights movement; however, Motley received almost no recognition for her role in making it successful. She was the LDF attorney who got the protesters out of jail and secured the court order to force the school board to reinstate all 1,081 black children who had been expelled for participating in the demonstration with King.

The marches that King led occurred before the end of the school year. In addition to being gassed, clubbed by police, hosed, attacked by dogs, and arrested, the children who had participated in the marches with King were expelled by the Birmingham school board. Their parents received letters from the Birmingham Board of Education notifying them that none of the students would graduate or be promoted to the next grade.[34]

Motley provided the following details about the march and the expulsion of the children:

> When the children appeared in a planned demonstration on Saturday morning, the city fathers did something totally unexpected. They retaliated by getting the Birmingham school board to expel from school eleven hundred students who allegedly had participated in the march. This was one week before graduation. Some of these students were poised to be graduating from eighth grade and go on to high school; some would be graduating from high school. . . . This school-board action greatly vexed these children and their parents. The parents wanted their children to graduate . . . and they let Dr. King and his associates know it. At this point, the city fathers had the upper hand. King and his associates were stymied as to what to do next.[35]

People in the black community, and especially the parents of the expelled students, were upset with King. Something had to be done very quickly to remedy the situation and get the children back in school immediately.

A late-night telephone call for help was made to Motley to get the children released from jail and the expulsion lifted. She was in Birmingham at the time working with Arthur Shores and Orzell Billingsley on a second case against the University of Alabama. They were seeking to enforce the court order that Judge Harlan Hobart Grooms had rendered in the Autherine Lucy case in 1955 and to compel the university to admit James Hood and Vivian Malone, two black students.[36] As always, Motley responded to the call for help "because again Martin Luther King had been arrested for parading without a permit," which was the favorite charge. "A permit to march would never be issued, so if they marched at all, it had to be done without a permit," she said.[37]

At 11:00 A.M. the next day, Motley went before Judge Clarence Allgood in the District Court for the Northern District of Alabama to get the protesters released from jail and to obtain a preliminary injunction against the expulsions and an order to force the school board to reinstate all the children. She was accompanied by Leroy Clark (a colleague at LDF), Shores, Billingsley, and local lawyers Peter Hall and Oscar Adams.[38] Motley argued the case. When the judge asked a sexist question—why she, a woman, was the only one arguing the case—

Motley replied, "Well, because I am the Legal Defense Fund attorney assigned to the case, and I have had prior experience in issues of this kind, and these local lawyers are not experienced in civil rights matters."[39]

Allgood lectured Motley about the use of the schoolchildren in the demonstrations, denied the motion, and refused to issue the injunction to prevent the children from being expelled. Although a transcript was required, none was made of the application for the preliminary injunction.[40]

Motley went to the court of appeals in Atlanta on May 22, 1963, where she obtained a temporary restraining order reinstating the children. The order was issued by Judge Elbert Tuttle, the chief justice of the Fifth Circuit Court of Appeals. Tuttle held that the children could not be expelled for engaging in legally permissible activities and that they had been illegally arrested for exercising their constitutional right. A panel of the Fifth Circuit reversed Allgood and entered a permanent injunction against the expulsions.[41]

The victory was obtained only after a great deal of drama, a race against the clock, and two airplane flights within five hours. Even before Motley went into court in Birmingham, she knew that Allgood was not going to enjoin the school board officials from expelling the students or order their reinstatement, so she had already called Tuttle and informed him that she would take a flight to Atlanta to appeal the anticipated adverse decision around 4:00 P.M. and arrive at the court of appeals around 5:00. Allgood apparently suspected the plan to fly from Birmingham to Atlanta to appeal his ruling, so he waited until after 2:00 P.M. to issue the order denying Motley's motion. He did not want her to have enough time to make the flight and get to court in Atlanta, where he knew the injunction would be issued and an order would be rendered to reinstate the students.[42]

After Allgood issued his ruling, Motley called Judge Tuttle in Atlanta again. He told her to take the 5:00 P.M. flight, the last flight of the day from Birmingham to Atlanta, and he would hear her argument at 7:00 P.M.[43] When she informed the lawyers for the school board that Judge Tuttle was going to hear the case that evening, they were stunned.[44]

Motley looked around at the activists in the courtroom for someone to serve as the plaintiff and to go with her on the flight from Birmingham to Atlanta. She selected Reverend Calvin Woods, the president of the Birmingham SCLC, the pastor of Shiloh Baptist Church, the former pastor of East End Baptist Church, and the father of Linda Cal Woods, an eleven-year-old fifth-grader at Booker T. Washington School who had been expelled.

Woods had participated in many protests against discrimination in Birmingham. He had been beaten and arrested many times and had been convicted and jailed for his leadership role in the boycott of Birmingham's segregated public bus system. Linda had not gotten permission to participate in the protest; she had sneaked out of school, hidden in the back of her father's Cadillac, and joined the marchers on Sixteenth Street after he parked and exited the car.[45]

When he was told by Motley that he would have to fly to Atlanta with her, Woods exclaimed that he had never been on a plane in his life and that he needed time to go home and tell his wife where he was going. Motley responded that there was not enough time for him to go home—that they had to leave right away.[46] She rushed out of court with Woods in tow, made the 5:00 P.M. flight, stopped by the office of Donald Hollowell (the local attorney in Atlanta), typed up her papers for the injunction, and argued the case in Judge Tuttle's courtroom at 7:00 P.M.[47]

Motley described the race against the clock that she, the other LDF lawyers, and Woods engaged in to get to the court of appeals. She commented as follows on the significance of the role that she and the other LDF lawyers played in the Birmingham campaign:

> I went to Atlanta with Leroy Clark and one of the local parents, Reverend Calvin Woods, who had been named as plaintiff. We were met by Donald Hollowell, our local counsel in Atlanta; we rushed to his office and hastily drew up the papers. He accompanied Leroy and me to court. . . . When we got to court at 7:00, it suddenly dawned on me that I was then the one in the eye of the storm. . . .
>
> I made our argument, which was that the young plaintiffs had been expelled without notice or hearing, a violation of due process. . . . Tuttle ruled that he would issue our requested injunction. . . . I was anxious to get back to Birmingham that night to advise Dr. King and his followers, who were gathered in one of the many black churches for their nightly meeting. I knew they would be there until 11:00 P.M. as they had been each night for months because I had been with them each night for about two weeks. With Judge Tutttle's permission, I left the courtroom to make the 9:00 P.M. flight. My opponents were still arguing with the judge when I left.
>
> I think it is fair to say that this was the most critical point in what we now call the Birmingham campaign. If Judge Tuttle had not held this extraordinary court session, Martin Luther King might have gone down in Birmingham. Instead, Tuttle's injunction revitalized King's efforts.[48]

Woods, Motley, and the other attorneys hurried to the airport, arrived back in Birmingham at 11:00 P.M., and went directly to the church where King and members of the black community were still discussing the march, the expulsion of the students, and tactics of the civil rights movement. "The black community was completely involved in the Birmingham campaign, and they had meetings every night," Motley recalled. "As these demonstrations went on . . . the people would just . . . move from church to church so that it would not appear that just one church was involved. They wanted the whole black community involved, which they did have."[49]

The expulsion of the students had presented a crisis situation in the black community in Birmingham and a critical situation for King as the leader of the civil rights movement. People, especially parents, blamed him for the school board's action. The black community "had gotten upset with Martin Luther King and his protest movement when it affected their children in this way. . . . They were turning against him and turning against the civil rights movement," said Motley.[50] So, she wanted to get back to Birmingham right away to let everybody know that the injunction had been issued, that all of the students would be going back to school the next day, and that those scheduled to graduate would do so.

The work that Motley and the LDF did in the Birmingham campaign was crucial for King and critical for the continual support of the civil rights movement by blacks in Birmingham.[51] Because of her success in the courts, King and the SCLC were able to announce that all the students who participated in the march would be reinstated in school, and King was therefore able to enjoy the continued support of the parents of the expelled students and the black community in Birmingham.

It was a significant turn of events; however, there was nothing at all in the local newspapers the next day about Motley's victory in forcing the school board to reinstate the children. She found out later that Judge Allgood in Birmingham "had called the local newspapers and suggested to them that they not publish anything about the granting of the injunction" and the court order to reinstate the students. "He didn't want the blacks to know that this victory had been achieved for them and that the children would be going back to school. If word didn't get to them, he figured . . . that they would continue to be annoyed with Martin King and not continue to support him."[52] Yet even though the newspapers did not print anything, blacks in Birmingham knew the injunction had been granted because it had been announced at the church meeting when Motley returned from Atlanta with the order from the court of appeals.

Motley reportedly said that her "greatest satisfaction came with the reinstatement" of the children in Birmingham.[53] She considered the victory over the Birmingham school board to be important because of its significance for King and his leadership of the civil rights movement. Joel confirmed his mother's view about the importance of the victory.

"My mother's most important case that I recall would be the Birmingham school case," he said, "which was really critical to Martin Luther King's progression as a leader of the civil rights movement. There, the children had been expelled from school, causing the parents to begin to lose faith in the movement, and getting them back into school . . . I think . . . she viewed as one of her major achievements."[54]

There was always a possibility that Motley could be injured or killed in Alabama. At all times during the Birmingham campaign she had bodyguards with her because the situation was very tense and dangerous.[55] She was always met at the airport by people who had been assigned to pick her up and escort her wherever she needed to go.

Hotels in Birmingham were segregated, so she usually stayed at the Gaston Motel, a black-owned and -operated motel. Arthur George Gaston was constantly worried that his hotel would be bombed, "because everything else was being bombed down there"—hence the city's nickname, Bombingham.[56]

Motley went to Birmingham many times after she won the case against the school board because King was always being arrested and jailed, and she was the attorney assigned to represent him. Many of the trips were taken to get King and other protesters out of jail. She would stay in Birmingham a day or two, go back to New York, and then go back to Birmingham a few days later. She prepared her court papers as much as she could in the office in New York and then took a night flight to Birmingham in order to get to the church before the meetings were over and to gather whatever she needed to appear in court the next day.

The exhaustive experience in the Birmingham campaign case was an example of Motley's tenacity and work ethic. In addition to being extremely intelligent and well trained, Motley possessed a "predacious capacity for plain old hard work driven by the justice of her causes and her commitment to her standards of excellence," said Drew Days.[57] Herbert Wright, the director for youth and college students at the NAACP, was often with Motley and witnessed the long hours she worked on a daily basis:

> People are not aware of the long hours that she . . . put in., Connie was an exemplification [of the hard work ethic] by her attitude and the workload that she took. . . . She would be there early in the morning, and you would see her late at night in the office, in the library with the staff preparing for the next case or preparing to leave for Mississippi or Texas or Louisiana or wherever the case may be. Her husband, Joel, came to pick her up every night, and he would say, "Honey, are you ready to go?" And she would say, "No, I gotta finish this brief or review this brief. I want to go over this brief, or I won't be able to come into the office tomorrow" or "I'll be going straight to the airport" to go to Mississippi or Louisiana or Georgia or wherever she had to go to represent the . . . plaintiffs [in the case] that she was handling at that particular time.[58]

The tenacity and the work ethic that Motley demonstrated in the school de-segregation cases and in representing King and the protesters in Atlanta and Birmingham proved to be important in other work that Motley performed. They were especially important in her representation of college student protesters and others who participated in sit-ins and freedom rides.

In the early 1960s college students joined the protest movement to end legal segregation and achieve full equality for blacks. They engaged in civil disobedience and demonstrations to force desegregation of lunch counters, restaurants, public transportation, theaters, museums, hotels, parks, swimming pools, beaches, courtrooms, and libraries.

The students organized sit-ins at segregated lunch counters and other public places. They also organized freedom rides to force desegregation of bus terminals and train stations to test federal enforcement of the Supreme Court ruling and laws that prohibited racial discrimination on buses that traveled from state to state—interstate transportation. The sit-ins and freedom rides mobilized blacks throughout the South and the country to protest racial segregation and convinced whites from the North to join the movement.

The sit-ins and freedom rides were catalytic events in the civil rights movement. Motley won cases that protected the right of the activists to engage in those protests. She also won the cases that set aside the arrests and convictions of those who participated in them. To a great extent, it was her success in the courtroom making it possible for protesters to continue the sit-ins and freedom rides that ultimately forced Congress to pass legislation that prohibited racial segregation in public accommodations—the Civil Rights Act of 1964 (the 1964 Act)—and achieve the goals of the civil rights movement.

"The Civil Rights Act of 1964 meant that Congress finally joined the executive and judicial branches in ending segregation and discrimination in America's public life," said Motley. "In short, the struggle for equal protection under the law had been won."[59]

The sit-in movement was sparked by the bold leadership of the Greensboro Four, college students "who dared to sit in at a drugstore or Woolworth's lunch counter and demand service" in North Carolina in 1960.[60] Around the same time that students were staging sit-ins in North Carolina, Diane Nash was leading a group of students in sit-ins in Nashville. Those students also attacked segregation at lunch counters and other places of public accommodation in Tennessee.[61]

The college students who staged the sit-ins knew that in *Brown* the court had decided that blacks had to be accorded equality with whites. They understood that *Brown* symbolized the federal government's recognition of its responsibility to protect blacks and to guarantee that they received equal treatment under the law.

The students also knew that they would be arrested and possibly jailed, but they didn't have any jobs to jeopardize or any fear of economic or other forms of reprisal from whites. They did not sit in at first-class restaurants where blacks generally could not afford to eat. Rather, they attacked "lunch counters in department stores and in Five and Tens in their hometown[s]," where their families and friends shopped, and in the college towns where they went to school, because they frequented those stores and bought a lot of their clothes and school supplies from them.[62]

"Every black child knew that when he went shopping on Saturday with Mama downtown to buy clothes," Motley said, "the white children could go to the lunch counter and have a hot dog and soda and ice cream, and the black children could not. And this was something which . . . black college students who grew up in the South were quite aware of, and so they were ready to do away with this indignity after the Supreme Court decision in *Brown*, and the groundswell for equality was taking shape."[63]

As the sit-in movement spread, thousands of students were arrested around the country. Bernard Lafayette was responsible for continuually filling the establishments in Nashville with new, replacement sit-in protesters as students were led out, arrested, and jailed.[64]

Within a relatively short period, Motley noted, the whole country "was engulfed in a wider desegregation struggle arising out of the freedom rider movement, which attacked segregation in transportation, and the sit-in movement, which attacked segregation at lunch counters and places of public accommodation." The LDF was "totally unprepared for these two major developments—that is, the spontaneous movement in the black community to do away with the indignity which blacks daily faced in just going to work on public transportation and the equally absurd indignity of not being able to get a hot dog when they went downtown to shop in the Five and Ten."[65] Taken by surprise, the LDF had to quickly realign its priorities and divert some of its legal resources to defend thousands of students who had been arrested, convicted, and jailed all over the country for participating in freedom rides and sit-ins. It also had to file lawsuits to knock down the state and local laws requiring segregation of public transportation, lunch counters, and public facilities.

Again Motley and her colleague Jack Greenberg were pressed into action; they represented students who had been arrested, convicted, and jailed. They argued cases to get the students out of jail so that the students could continue their protest actions. They took a series of cases to the Supreme Court that became known as "the sit-in cases."[66]

As convictions mounted for thousands of participants in sit-ins and freedom rides, the question arose of what would happen to all these pending convictions. The question was answered when the sit-in cases were won in the Supreme Court and Congress was forced to pass the 1964 Act to end de jure segregation and create equal rights for blacks in American society. The 1964 Act was predicated not only on the Fourteenth Amendment but also on the Interstate Commerce Clause, which empowers Congress to regulate all aspects of interstate commerce.

As soon as the 1964 Act was passed, Motley petitioned the Supreme Court to set aside *all* the convictions that had resulted from the sit-ins because the establishments used channels of interstate commerce in their businesses. The 1964 Act provided that if a facility or business used channels of interstate commerce, it could not engage in racial discrimination. The lunch counters and restaurants where the sit-ins occurred relied upon interstate commerce to receive shipments of food and other goods for the inventory and products to be served to customers. The buses the protesters rode on in the freedom rides traveled on interstate roads. Motley argued that neither the sit-in arrests nor their convictions could stand in light of Congress's enactment of the 1964 Act. The Supreme Court justices agreed and overturned *all* the convictions.

Herbert Wright assisted Motley with the sit-in cases. "Working with youth and college students meant that we were fully involved in the major campaigns and activities to try and bring about freedom and equality," he said. "Many of the civil rights activities . . . were started by our youth and college groups. . . . The activities that kicked off the sit-ins that started in Greensboro, North Carolina, were started by young people who were members . . . of the NAACP."[67]

The mass movement of student sit-ins and other forms of direct action protest was organized by students who were "disillusioned with the snail's pace" of desegregation and frustrated with "the deliberate thwarting of justice in all deliberate speed." The NAACP experienced difficulty in controlling the activities of its young members "in the rapidly shifting civil rights terrain." They wanted to be on the "direct-action frontlines," and they "pushed well past the adult leadership of old-line civil rights organizations" like the NAACP to bring about social change more quickly.[68]

Officials of the NAACP on the national level, as well as male lawyers at the LDF, initially opposed the students' sit-in actions. Motley, in contrast, was quick to defend them. Thurgood Marshall was slow to support the students, and Roy Wilkins, the former executive director of the NAACP, never came around to supporting their actions. Wright believed that the men were concerned about the appearance of the NAACP supporting attempts to restrain trade.

Discord developed between the student and adult members of the NAACP when the students staged their sit-ins. Wright commented as follows on the disagreement:

> There was a conflict between our youth and our adult units. There was a belief among some of our lawyers—the late Thurgood Marshall, who was our general counsel—and others who were worried that there might be

an interpretation that if our youths were to initiate some of these activities it might be construed that the NAACP was attempting to restrain trade, and that created a problem for us. So many of our young people undertook the activities on their own or through their youth counsels without the identification of the NAACP.[69]

Although Marshall, the male lawyers at the LDF, and the national leaders of the NAACP opposed the students' actions and were hesitant to lend support to them, Motley courageously stepped up and represented the students from the very beginning. Her agency in the sit-in cases was critical to the success of the civil rights movement. Her work in trial courts, appellate courts, and the Supreme Court on behalf of the students who were arrested made it possible for them to sustain their protest actions, accelerate the end of de jure segregation, and force radical change to take place in the United States.

Time after time, Constance Baker Motley was the lawyer sent to the Jim Crow South to represent students fighting to integrate colleges and universities and to represent Martin Luther King, sit-in protesters, freedom riders, and other activists when they were arrested and jailed. She was also the one sent to Mississippi to work with Medgar Evers and the NAACP. She even spent a night under guard at his home just before Evers was assassinated in June 1963.[70]

Motley was sent on assignments because she was a woman and because of Marshall's joking theory, noted earlier, that black women were safer in the South than black men because all white men had had black nannies. Marshall may have nurtured Motley and helped her develop into an excellent lawyer; however, his action in constantly sending her to the South could be classified as discrimination on the basis of sex since her femaleness was clearly a factor in the assignments.

As we also noted in chapter 4, black women were not safer in the South; as well as being arrested and jailed because of their civil rights activities, they were harassed, brutally beaten within inches of their lives, sexually assaulted and raped, pistol-whipped, shot, and tortured. Fannie Lou Hamer had permanent injuries from the beatings she received: the loss of her left eye, irreparable damage to her kidneys, and the exacerbation of a limp that she had from childhood polio.[71] The homes of Daisy Bates and Carlotta Walls LaNier were bombed, set on fire, and riddled with bullets. The black women who organized the Montgomery Bus Boycott were also victims of violence. Jo Ann Robinson barely escaped serious injuries when rocks and bombs were thrown in her home and acid was poured over her car.[72] Black female freedom riders were beaten and strip-searched while confined at Parchman Farm (Mississippi State Penitentiary), a notorious maximum security facility where executions were carried out.[73] Motley too was exposed to acts of violence and danger in much of her work in the South.

Charles Ogletree—a law professor at Harvard University, the founder of the

Charles Hamilton Houston Institute for Race and Justice, and a Motley family friend—spoke about the fact that Motley was constantly required to leave her family in the North and travel extensively to dangerous places in the South to represent LDF clients while the male attorneys remained in the comfort and safety of the LDF office in the North. Referring to William T. Coleman, an LDF president who worked alongside Motley and other attorneys during the civil rights movement, Ogletree stated, "Bill Coleman sort of understated it when he commented that the guys at the LDF said, 'Let Connie do it. Send Connie there [South]. Maybe they won't hurt her.'"[74] And Coleman himself admitted, "You know, we had tough problems, and she'd go South and she would tell us how to work out the problems. We'd sit in New York or Philadelphia and talk from there. And I sometimes felt guilty that I didn't have the courage to face them in the South the way she did."[75]

Herbert Wright often traveled with Motley and was an eyewitness to some of the dangerous conditions she worked under and the precautions that were taken to try to protect her. "Connie, in her various trips to Mississippi to try to get James Meredith into Ole Miss, of course was always in constant danger . . . because of the major objection to integration of the schools in that state. . . . We were aware of that, and we took precautions to keep her as safe as humanly possible," he said.[76]

As already noted, because Motley and the NAACP staff could not stay in hotels in the South, they always looked for blacks in the community who were not afraid to have them in their homes and provide protection for them, and "members of local chapters of the NAACP would stand guard outside all night and watch the houses" where they slept to provide protection for them.[77] Wright further explained, "We couldn't count on, unfortunately, the local police to provide the security needed, nor in some instances could we count on the local members of the FBI, because often they were in cahoots with the local police."[78]

Being a lawyer for the LDF was obviously a dangerous occupation. Regarding Motley's experiences driving throughout the South, Drew Days described how she would be "looking over her shoulder, fearful that she was being followed by racist members of the Klan who might do her in."[79]

Motley rarely talked about the danger of her civil rights work with her son, Joel, while he was a child because she didn't want to frighten him. Although she didn't tell him a lot about what was going on, it was obvious to him that what she was involved in was tense and difficult, because she would sometimes be away from home for ten days at a time. In subsequent years, when he was older, Motley talked with Joel about instances in which she was particularly frightened that something bad could happen to her. One incident occurred when she and her secretary were traveling at night from one courthouse to another and were being followed by a car. "The other thing that brought the danger home," Joel said, "was when she talked about the assassination of Medgar Evers. . . . And of course, Medgar was shot right in front of [his] house. After that, she left the Legal Defense Fund."[80]

Motley often talked about mourning Medgar Evers and about the shrubbery around his house. She warned him to do something about the bushes, because somebody could hide in them, come from behind them, and ambush him. As she feared and warned, Evers was assassinated with a high-powered rifle in his front yard by someone hiding behind those bushes.[81]

6
Desegregating America, Case by Case, in the Supreme Court

Undoubtedly, the dream of every litigating lawyer is to argue a case before the Supreme Court and win. Most lawyers never get the chance. Arguing several significant cases before that court and winning is, indeed, a rarity. This opportunity earned me a place in the history of the Supreme Court. I may have been the first black woman in modern times to argue before the Supreme Court.

—Constance Baker Motley, *Equal Justice under Law*

Constance Baker Motley handled a large number of cases that were appealed. As a result, she was often inundated with work to get cases ready to be heard in the Supreme Court. She had to do the time-consuming tasks of preparing the record for the appeal, writing the brief to be filed, and preparing to argue the case.

The LDF and the NAACP as a whole did not limit themselves to challenging desegregation in education, housing, voting rights, and public accommodations. They also took cases challenging discrimination and the unequal treatment of blacks in the criminal justice system. Motley argued and won criminal cases, including a death penalty case she tried with James Nabrit III, a colleague at the LDF. Nabrit wrote the following about his experience working with her:

> I worked with Constance Baker Motley on various occasions during the time she was a lawyer for the NAACP Legal Defense and Educational Fund. I think that Mrs. Motley first became well-known to the public in the 1950s and 1960s as the lawyer who represented several black students who were admitted to previously all-white state universities in the south. Autherine Lucy, Charlayne Hunter, Hamilton Holmes, James Meredith, Harvey Gantt, Vivian Malone, and James Hood were her clients in various courts. Her spectacular efforts in these cases, defeating a series of officials "who stood in the schoolhouse doors" trying to block black applicants, won her a national reputation for excellence as a lawyer. She was indomitable.

My own closest work with Mrs. Motley came in a less well-known effort. We successfully represented an Alabama death row inmate named Charles Clarence Hamilton before the US Supreme Court. Hamilton had been convicted of an Alabama capital crime (burglary in the night with intent to ravish), despite never having touched the crime victim. . . . In *Hamilton v. Alabama*, Mrs. Motley won for our client, who had no lawyer at his arraignment, which was deemed to be a crucial procedural stage in the case, even though he had a lawyer later. The Supreme Court victory led to the saving of Hamilton's life after further proceedings.[1]

Nabrit described Motley's demeanor in court and the high regard the justices had for her. "I have a recollection of Mrs. Motley's great dignity and presence as she argued that and other cases in the U.S. Supreme Court," he said, and he remembered "the relish that Chief Justice Earl Warren seemed to take in addressing her as 'Senator' Motley, after her election to the New York State Senate. It was clear that the Chief Justice of the United States was impressed by Constance Baker Motley."[2]

The cases that Motley argued in the Supreme Court were all important in the advancement of civil rights and equality for all, the goal of the civil rights movement. They are summarized in this chapter.

On October 17, 1961, Motley argued *Hamilton v. State of Alabama,* her first case in the Supreme Court.[3] It was, as Nabrit wrote, a criminal case that involved the right of a defendant to have counsel at his arraignment in a capital case. All her colleagues at the LDF were there to back her up and give her support. The night before her Supreme Court argument, Motley had an oral argument practice session at Howard University. Law professors asked her questions similar to those they assumed the Supreme Court justices would ask so that she got a good workout. The next day, the Supreme Court treated her well and rendered a unanimous decision in her favor.[4]

The issue Motley raised on appeal was whether a defendant in a capital case was entitled to counsel at every step of the proceeding, including the arraignment, or if the right to counsel was limited to just the trial. She argued that Hamilton had been denied his Fourteenth Amendment right of due process because he had not been represented by counsel at his arraignment. The Supreme Court ruled that the defendant in a criminal case was entitled to counsel at his arraignment and at every stage of the proceeding and reversed Hamilton's conviction. The ruling was very important in establishing the right of all defendants to have legal representation at every stage of a criminal case.

The second case Motley tried in the Supreme Court was argued in 1962. That case, *Turner v. City of Memphis* involved a plaintiff who was refused nonsegregated service in a restaurant with seating arranged so that blacks and whites were physically separated.[5] The restaurant was operated by a business that leased space from the City of Memphis in the municipal airport, and it followed a state law that required racially segregated seating in eating facilities. Motley attacked the state regulation on constitutional grounds and sought an injunction to permanently prohibit the city of Memphis and its tenant, the restaurant in the airport, from operating racially segregated eating facilities and bathrooms. The Supreme Court accepted her argument, holding that the state regulation requiring racial segregation in publicly operated facilities violated the Fourteenth Amendment and was unconstitutional. The case was remanded to the district court with directions to enter an injunction permanently banning racial discrimination in the restaurant at the airport. That case was important in the fight for equality; it set the precedent that made it possible for black travelers and visitors to use fully integrated facilities in an airport.

On November 6, 1962, Motley went to the Supreme Court again and argued *Gober v. City of Birmingham*, a student sit-in case.[6] This time she challenged an ordinance in Birmingham that required racial segregation in public eating places and the conviction of ten black students who violated the ordinance by engaging in a sit-in to protest the discrimination. The students had been convicted of criminal trespassing on private property in state court because they sat at the all-white lunch counters in department stores, requested service, and failed to leave when they were asked to do so. The Supreme Court reversed the convictions and held that the ordinance requiring racial segregation in publicly operated facilities violated the Fourteenth Amendment and was unconstitutional.

Motley argued a related case concerning sit-ins in Birmingham. That case, *Shuttlesworth v. City of Birmingham*, involved two black ministers who had provided counseling to students who staged sit-ins at lunch counters.[7] The ministers had not accompanied the students to the lunch counters or participated in the sit-ins. "Nevertheless, the ministers were convicted in the Alabama court of aiding and abetting trespass" because "they had counseled the students beforehand," Motley said.[8] The Supreme Court reversed the convictions. It held that the ministers' convictions had to be set aside because the convictions of the students they allegedly assisted had been reversed in the *Gober* case; therefore, there could be no convictions for aiding and abetting.

Watson v. City of Memphis involved black residents of Memphis who brought an action against the city seeking declaratory and injunctive relief to require immediate desegregation of municipal parks and all recreational facilities that were either owned or operated by the city.[9] The District Court for the Western District of Tennessee denied the plaintiffs' request. It ordered the city to submit a plan providing for desegregation of the parks and recreational facilities over a period of several years. The Sixth Circuit Court of Appeals affirmed the district court's decision. Motley appealed to the Supreme Court, which unanimously reversed the district court decision. It held that the delay in implementing the constitutionally required desegregation of public facilities, over a period of years rather than immediately, could not be justified in the absence of the city showing compelling reasons for the delay. The victory in that case opened previously all-white public parks and recreational facilities to blacks and whites on an equal basis.

In *Calhoun v. Latimer,* Motley represented plaintiffs who sought to desegregate public schools in Atlanta.[10] The District Court for the Northern District of Georgia ruled against her and refused to order the schools to admit black students. After the Fifth Circuit Court of Appeals affirmed the district court's ruling, she appealed the case to the Supreme Court. When she tried the case in Atlanta in 1958, the trial court decided that "segregation in the school system was voluntary on the part of blacks and whites," and it came up with "the most unreasonable plan one could devise—a grade a year plan [for desegregation of the schools] starting in the twelfth grade," said Motley.[11] During oral arguments in the Supreme Court, the attorney for the Atlanta school board advised the justices that the plan Motley characterized as unreasonable (because it would take twelve years to integrate the schools) had been modified, and that under the new plan students could freely transfer between schools in order to desegregate them and end the dual segregated school systems immediately. The Supreme Court remanded the case to the district court so that it could determine the impact of the school board's free transfer plan and whether it complied with the mandate in *Brown v. Board of Education* to desegregate public schools *with* "all deliberate speed."

In *Bouie v. City of Columbia,* two black students were convicted of trespassing for staging a sit-in and refusing to leave a booth in the luncheonette section of a drugstore.[12] The store had a policy that permitted blacks to shop in the store but not to be seated and served in the luncheonette located inside the store. After the black students sat down, a store employee put a NO TRESPASSING sign up and asked them to leave the booth they were sitting in. The students refused to leave; they were arrested and charged with breach of the peace and criminal trespassing but were convicted only of trespassing. (The relevant South Carolina statute made it a crime—trespassing—for a person to enter the property of another *after* being notified that the entry was prohibited.) The Supreme Court reversed the trespassing convictions because the students had not been notified not to enter before they entered the luncheonette and sat in the booth. Instead, the notice (the NO TRESPASSING sign) had not been put up until after they had entered the premises and sat in the booth. The court held that punishment of the students for a crime that they did not have prior notice of—an ex post facto crime—would constitute a violation of due process under the Fourteenth Amendment. The case was decided by the Supreme Court two days after the Senate passed the Civil Rights Act of 1964, which prohibited racial segregation in all public accommodations.

Barr v. City of Columbia was another sit-in case argued by Motley.[13] Similar to the facts in *Bouie*, black students were arrested and charged with breach of the peace after they sat down and waited for service at a lunch counter in a store that had a policy of permitting only whites to sit and eat. The Supreme Court cited its decision in *Bouie* and reversed the convictions. It held that the students had been polite, quiet, and peaceful from the time they entered the store until they left and that there was no evidence to support the breach of peace convictions.

Hamm v. City of Rock Hill and *Lupper v. State of Arkansas* were two sit-in cases in which the defendants had been convicted of trespassing.[14] The Supreme Court granted certiorari (a call for records) in order to review the decisions of the state courts and consolidated the cases. Jack Greenberg argued the *Hamm* case and Motley argued the *Lupper* case.

Hamm's sit-in occurred at a lunch counter that restricted service to whites only in a South Carolina variety store. Arthur Hamm Jr. remained seated when he was refused service because of his race. *Lupper*'s sit-in occurred in a mezzanine-level tearoom that restricted service to whites only in an Arkansas department store. Frank Lupper also remained seated when he was refused service because of his race and was requested to leave.

Both Hamm and Lupper were arrested at the stores where their sit-ins occurred. They were prosecuted and convicted of violating their states' trespassing statutes. Both argued that their Fourteenth Amendment rights had been violated and that their convictions had to be set aside because the Civil Rights Act of 1964 prohibited segregation in places of public accommodation. The Supreme Court agreed and overturned their convictions. It held that the lunch counter and tearoom in the stores that offered service to interstate travelers were places of public accommodation within the meaning of the act.

Motley's victory in the *Lupper* case led to the reversal of all the arrests and convictions in all the sit-in cases. "It was, without a doubt, the most difficult case I argued," she said. "If it had been lost, thousands of students involved in sit-in cases pending in the South would have remained in the clutches of angry local police, prosecutors, and jailers who had just lost the war in the Congress. The Civil Rights Act of 1964 meant that Congress finally joined the executive and judicial branches in ending segregation and discrimination in America's public life. In short, the struggle for equal protection under the law had been won."[15]

In December 1964 Motley argued *Swain v. Alabama,* her tenth and last case at the Supreme Court—and the only one she lost.[16] She objected to an Alabama prosecutor's use of his peremptory challenges to remove all black jury-duty candidates who had been called to try the defendant, Robert Swain, a black man, for the alleged attempt to rape a white woman in Talladega County, Alabama.

The use of peremptory challenges to exclude blacks from juries was a widespread practice in the South at the time.[17]

Prospective jurors can be excluded from juries by two methods. One method is a challenge for cause—if, for example, the person is not a citizen, does not understand and speak English, or is a convicted felon. The other method is a peremptory challenge, in which a lawyer has the right to exclude or remove a person from a jury simply because the lawyer personally believes that he or she should not be selected. When peremptory challenge is used, the lawyer does not have to disclose the reason for wanting to exclude or remove a person from a jury.

Motley lost the *Swain* case when the Supreme Court affirmed the trial court's ruling and upheld the use of peremptory challenges to remove all the black jurors in the case. Twenty years later, in *Batson v. Kentucky,* the *Swain* case was reversed.[18]

In a 2004 interview Motley applauded the reversal of *Swain* and claimed a victory in all ten of the cases she argued in the Supreme Court. "The tenth case I won 20 years later . . . when the court adopted my view that it was a violation of equal protection for prosecutors in criminal cases to use their peremptory challenges to get rid of all of the blacks on a jury panel," she said.[19] Continuing from the quote that opens this chapter, Motley shared her perspective about being the first black woman to argue before the Supreme Court:

> It was an opportunity I never expected to have when I initially contemplated law as a profession. I must acknowledge, of course, that I also coincided with history, and I have never lost sight of that fact. In the twentieth century, the rights of black Americans under the Constitution were vindicated, and the federal judiciary emerged as the primary forum for recognizing these rights. I must also acknowledge my good fortune in having had the educational training and litigation experience with the LDF, whose victories they really were.[20]

Characterizing Motley as a brilliant woman and a wonderful lawyer, Drew Days commented, "Now there is no contesting the fact that Judge Motley, during her . . . years with the NAACP Legal Defense Fund, was one of the finest lawyers in America." He added that she was recognized by Supreme Court justices as being a superb lawyer and that Justice William O. Douglas, in particular, praised her as "an outstanding lawyer who mastered the facts, mastered the record, and also mastered the art of trial advocacy and the best argument the other side could make." Days quoted Justice Douglas as saying that "of all the lawyers who appeared before the Supreme Court," he would "probably have to rank her among the top 10."[21]

7

The Transition from
Activist Movement Lawyer

The major legal battles were over. . . . I thought I should look for other areas
in which to practice law or use my legal training.
                                        —Constance Baker Motley, *Equal Justice under Law*

After almost twenty years at the LDF (from 1945 as a law clerk and from 1946
through 1964 as a staff attorney), Constance Baker Motley made the transition from an activist movement lawyer to political office. The stress of constant
travel and extended periods away from her family, the emotional toll of dealing
with taunts and hostility directed at her from angry mobs, and the insults she
endured from having to be served in segregated restaurants and confined to segregated public accommodations because she was black influenced her decision.

The assassination of Medgar Evers, whom she had worked very closely with
on NAACP cases, was also a significant factor in her decision. "She looked back
on those years [and] said that Medgar's assassination was one of the things that
really made her feel that continuing on would be especially difficult," said Joel,
her son, "not just because they had worked closely together, but because of the
particularly violent . . . way in which he had been killed. . . . I think that when
Medgar was killed she really decided that twenty years of going to the South had
become just not enough but almost too much and it was time to move on."[1] By
then Motley had devoted a substantial portion of her professional life to litigating civil rights cases in the South, and she believed that it was time for a career
change. She decided to embark on a career in politics.

Thurgood Marshall's decision a few years earlier to pass her over and support
Jack Greenberg to replace him as director counsel of the LDF when he left to become a judge on the Second Circuit Court of Appeals also influenced Motley's
decision to leave the organization. She had begun her tenure at the LDF before
Greenberg arrived; however, Marshall chose Greenberg as his successor. Motley

recalled, "Medgar Evers, the NAACP field secretary in Mississippi, was so certain I would be [Marshall's] successor that he had posters printed to this effect announcing a public meeting in Mississippi at which I was the main speaker. . . . The resentment among the NAACP rank and file" to the selection of Greenberg over Motley was muted, however, and remained private among those at the LDF and the NAACP as a whole.[2]

It could be argued that Marshall's decision was an act of sex discrimination. Some may characterize his choice as evidence of the pattern of sexism that was consistent with denying black women formal titles and positions as leaders of black churches and male-dominated civil rights organizations.

Greenberg, however, rejected the view that Marshall or any of the male attorneys at the LDF were sexist or that Motley was discriminated against because she was a woman. He said that she was treated the same as all the other lawyers at the LDF. "Connie . . . was like any other lawyer," he insisted. "She had her strengths and her unique qualities, but I don't think that the fact that she was a woman played any part in anybody else's perception of her. . . . Everybody had a good working relationship with Thurgood, and she did, too. And she had a good working relationship with me and all her other colleagues."[3]

Motley was sensitive to the argument that sexism played a role in Marshall's decision to pass her over. She refuted the sexism charge, defended Marshall's selection of Greenberg as his successor, and revealed details about the internal discord and politics that may have led to Marshall's action.

A feud developed between Marshall and Robert Carter, who had been Marshall's chief assistant since about 1949. Carter had become quite dissatisfied with Marshall's leadership of the LDF because he believed that Marshall was spending too much time visiting NAACP branches and raising funds and was neglecting the legal work, which fell on Carter. Marshall was aware of Carter's view and was under the impression that Motley supported Carter's campaign to oust him, but she did not. She said that Carter had not confided in her about his plans. Because of his feud with Carter, Marshall may have "moved quickly to maneuver Jack Greenberg into the position as his successor," Motley explained. "Greenberg's installation came with such swiftness that there was no time for the opposition to mobilize."[4]

Motley believed that Marshall's reason for promoting Greenberg as his successor was partly based on financial concerns. The LDF was in great need of funds to finance its legal work, and Greenberg, who was white, had the support of most of the largest contributors to the LDF, all of whom were also white. In addition, Greenberg had the approval of the LDF board of directors for the position. Marshall's decision, said Motley, was based on merit, and the only opposition to Greenberg's selection as Marshall's successor would have been based on the fact that he was white, because his credentials were impeccable. She acknowledged, however, that, "Thurgood also had difficulty with the idea of a woman in a leadership role in a male world" and that since "the women's rights movement of the 1970s had not yet emerged," she had no female supporters other than New York Congresswoman Bella Abzug.[5]

In the 1960s, when Motley became a political actor, women held a marginal position in politics. "What distinguished women from men as political actors was their absence in all but token numbers from the visible, central seats of decision-making," noted Susan Hartmann. Politics was still considered to be for men and not for women. "Sex role socialization continued to define politics as a man's world and to discourage women from careers that typically provided stepping stones to political leadership. Those women who overcame such barriers to political aspiration still faced male reluctance to share power and popular misgivings about the propriety and capability of women for high office."[6]

The cases that Motley won during the civil rights movement opened doors for women—both black and white—in all fields and endeavors, including political careers. They helped transform the possibilities for women in politics, and that "afforded a broad scope for women's participation and leadership, especially at the grassroots level."[7]

In the South, in particular, it was largely black female activists who worked and led grassroots campaigns to end racial segregation in local communities, organized voter registration drives, and recruited the masses to participate in and support the civil rights movement. Motley not only represented many of those women during her career as a civil rights lawyer but also saw firsthand the impact that qualified and devoted leaders could have on initiating change and improving the lives of the masses.

Motley "understood that once the walls were torn down, once segregation had been largely if not totally eliminated, there were other challenges, substantial challenges, and those challenges largely involved economic and political empowerment of African Americans," said Douglas Schoen, a political consultant and historian who was familiar with Motley's transition to political office.[8] She had developed an interest in those issues and had acquired training as a political leader during the period she was unable to attend college because of a lack of financial resources.

While doing her work in the South, Motley had observed that politics and issues that affected the black community were largely under the control of black ministers. She respected and had confidence in Martin Luther King and the other ministers she had represented; however, she believed that lawyers and qualified leaders from other professions should get involved in politics and the representation of the black community. She decided that she was qualified and should enter politics.

After she made her decision, Motley ran for office, was elected, and in 1964 became the first black woman to serve in the New York State Senate. "When I learned . . . that the state senate job would be only part-time . . . and that I could still work for the LDF," she said, "I decided to run for the seat because it would broaden my experience. I had been with the LDF for eighteen years. The march on Washington the previous August had brought on that perennial feeling, which I had had many times since 1954, that the major legal battles were over. . . . I thought I should look for other areas in which to practice law or use my legal training. Moreover, I had been passed over for the top spot at LDF."[9]

In 1965 Motley ran for two more offices: she became the first woman to sit on the New York Board of Estimate and the first woman ever, black or white, to serve as the Manhattan Borough president. All three political parties—Republican, Democratic, and Liberal—endorsed her for borough president, a position in which she wielded enormous influence and power.[10] A *New York Times* editorial "noted in 1965 that Motley, a Democrat, had received the endorsement of the Liberal and Republican Parties, calling her 'a person of such unusual character that color became an irrelevancy in her candidacy.'"[11]

Douglas Schoen recalled that Motley ran in and won three elections in two years in which she was opposed by Congressman Adam Clayton Powell and other black male leaders in Harlem—reform Democrats who had been the champions of progress for blacks in the 1950s and 1960s.[12] Despite their opposition, Motley was elected and quickly became a political leader in New York and the highest-ranking African American woman in US politics.

As a movement lawyer, Motley represented the interests of blacks; however, when she became an elected official, she represented all her constituents. Throughout her two-year career in politics, Schoen said, "she was absolutely consistent in making it clear that while she was going to stand up and speak for African Americans, she would in no way be a champion of only African Americans. . . . In one of her speeches, she inserted with an asterisk that she was a champion of all races in order to emphasize her concern about all people."[13]

An article about her election to the New York State Senate entitled "Going Upstate" reads, "Mrs. Constance Baker Motley, 42, first Negro woman elected to State Senate, is sworn in by Mayor Wagner at City Hall. She . . . vowed to fight for the cause of all people."[14] In one of her speeches as Manhattan Borough president, Motley spoke of her goal to rehabilitate and renovate Harlem; however, she also emphasized that she wanted Harlem to be a center of life in New York City and a vibrant community for all New Yorkers.[15] During her tenure as borough president she worked tirelessly to revitalize the inner city and improve urban housing and public schools.[16]

After a tumultuous two years in politics, in January 1966 Motley "received a call from the White House instructing her, without further explanation . . . to appear at the East Gate on a particular day, at a particular time."[17] She did as directed. Years later she remarked that when she and her husband arrived at the White House, she was happy that she was wearing her favorite black dress and a new hat, because President Lyndon B. Johnson informed her that he was nominating her to be the first woman to serve as a judge in the District Court for the Southern District of New York, the largest federal trial bench in the United States. The appointment was the culmination of episodes of sex discrimination and much political theater.

Originally Johnson had planned to submit Motley's name to the US Senate to fill the vacancy on the Second Circuit Court of Appeals when Thurgood Marshall left to become the US solicitor general. There was so much opposition to her appointment, however, that Johnson did not move forward with the plan. The opposition came from Wall Street lawyers, primarily white men, as well as from male judges. The men objected to the appointment because she was a woman, and a position on the court of appeals had never been filled by a woman.[18] The appointment, noted one observer, "sparked a level of opposition among some federal jurists that rivaled the race-based resistance of southern senators."[19]

Motley believed that the opposition was led by J. Edward Lombard, the chief justice of the Second Circuit Court of Appeals. "Lombard and others on the Second Circuit didn't want any woman in this milieu," she said. "New York was the real power center of the whole circuit, which also includes Connecticut and Vermont, because there you had all the great commercial cases and so forth. Their attitude, pure and simple, was that a woman had no business being there."[20]

Opposition to Motley's judicial appointment also came from Mississippi Senator James Eastland, Southern Democrats, and other elected officials in Washington and beyond. She had alienated many of them when she won desegregation suits against states they represented while she was at the LDF.

While her nomination to the District Court for the Southern District of New York was pending, the judicial screening committee from the New York City Bar Association had one gender-based and demeaning question to ask Motley: whether she would sit on the bench in one of those bright flowered dresses that women wore.[21]

Despite the strong opposition, Motley was confirmed to the judiciary nine months after Johnson's appointment. "She was named to become an appeals court judge," but the fierce opposition to her appointment "forced a compromise, placing her on the district court" instead.[22] Motley fought hard for her appointment; she prevailed and became the first black woman in the country to be appointed as a federal judge.

In addition to opposition from Southern senators, Robert F. Kennedy, the senator from New York, had initially submitted Motley's name for a judicial appointment but then withdrew his support for her because of a political disagreement between them. Joel related the following story about the politics that surrounded his mother's judicial nomination and appointment and Kennedy's withdrawal of his support:

> In 1964, my mother was elected to the state senate, which was then a part-time position, so she was still at the Legal Defense Fund and at the state senate part-time. [The year] 1964 was also [when] Lyndon Johnson was elected president, and the landslide had the effect of giving Democrats control of the state senate, which they had not had for many years.... And in the course of organizing the [New York] senate after the election, Bobby Kennedy was elected [US] senator from New York, and he actually submitted my mother's name to the White House to be a federal judge. After that the struggle over leadership of the state senate got underway.... Bobby Kennedy had a candidate, and the minority leader, Joe Zaresky, who was a state senator from the Bronx, had been in line to become the majority leader.... Kennedy was pushing someone else, and my mother thought Zaresky really deserved it because he had been the minority leader for so long.... And she voted for him and he won. After that, her nomination to the federal bench went nowhere and she became borough president of Manhattan....
>
> One day, she saw Bobby Kennedy at a political event and invited him for a ride in her limousine and asked him whatever happened to her judicial nomination—to which he gave no response.... In the White House, others had seen her nomination and brought it to the president's attention, and eventually Lyndon Johnson himself nominated her to be on the bench.... When she went to the White House to meet the president, he told her that he had seen her name come across his desk and wondered about it and decided on his own to find out more about it. So he [Johnson] called Martin Luther King and Whitney Young and said, "Who is Constance Baker Motley?" They said, "Oh, she's wonderful, and she's done all this for us and would make a fabulous judge." He said he decided to go ahead and put her name in himself....
>
> Those of you who remember the history will remember that Lyndon Johnson and Bobby Kennedy were not always the best of friends, so after he [Johnson] told her this story, he said to his secretary, "See if you can get Senator Kennedy on the phone," which she did.... The president took the phone and he said, "Bobby, this is Lyndon. I have Judge Motley here, and I thought you would want to be the first one to congratulate her." He handed the phone to her and she felt a bit awkward but got through it.[23]

After being appointed as a judge, Motley had to attend the school for new federal judges in Berkeley, California. She was disrespected and marginalized by the chairman of the group, another federal judge, who introduced each new judge at the meeting. "In doing so," Motley explained, "he told those assembled about how great each new judge was, how each had distinguished himself in the law. When it came to introducing me, he said simply that I had been on the board of the United Church Women, and I had been on the board of the YMCA, and that was it."[24]

Upon the completion of judge school, Motley took her place as the only female judge on the District Court for the Southern District of New York. In addition to being the only female judge and the only black judge, she was the only black professional and the only woman who worked in the federal courthouse. For many years, there was only one black male employee, and he worked there in a nonprofessional position.

The male judges apparently welcomed Motley as a colleague when it came to assignments and adjusting to the work of the court; however, she was a victim of sexism in other ways. For instance, even after she joined the court, the male judges continued to eat meals and hold meetings that she had to attend at places that admitted and served males only.[25]

A specific example of this sexism was the annual judges' dinner, which was held in a restaurant that did not admit or serve women. Also, for the first ten years or so after her appointment to the court, the judges had a dinner every two to three months at a country club that barred women from membership.

"When I arrived [became a judge], the judges realized that they might have a problem with my admission for the dinner meetings because the club had the policy of not admitting women to social functions that took place above the first floor," wrote Motley. "The dinners were always held in a room on the second floor. . . . Sidney Sugarman, who became the chief judge of our court right after I was sworn in . . . told me a few years later that in order to get me on the second floor, he had told a little white lie to the powers that be—that I was the secretary and therefore had to come to the dinner meeting to take notes" for the judges.[26]

Motley commented on a specific meeting that she was invited to attend shortly after she became a judge. It too was held at a club that was not open to women. "I was invited to attend a meeting of the Lawyers Club as a newly appointed judge. . . . The club's meeting room was on the twentieth floor of a building near the courthouse on lower Broadway," she said. "When I got on the elevator the day of the luncheon, I said to the young white male operator: 'Twenty, please.' He responded, 'No women on twenty.' When I told him I was a guest of the Lawyers Club, he took me to twenty-one, where I got off. There was no one there. The room was dark. The elevator man must have then notified a club member, because soon thereafter someone came up the stairs from the twentieth floor and fetched me."[27]

Despite these obstacles in her early career as a judge, Motley settled in and became an excellent jurist. She took Roberta Thomas—her trusted secretary with whom she had had a long, rich, and complex relationship—to the district court as her secretary. Their professional and personal association dated back to Motley's days working on desegregation cases at the LDF. Thomas had often accompanied Motley on her trips to the South so that she could type documents that had to be filed in court on an emergency basis.

Law clerks were hired to assist Motley with her work as a federal judge. Two of them provided accounts of their observations of her and their experiences working in her chambers. One was Laura Taylor Swain, currently a judge herself in the Southern District of New York, who was one of the clerks at the time. The other was James Farmer, the chief of the Criminal Division of the US Attorney's Office in Boston.

Motley had such high regard for Derrick Bell, her former colleague at the LDF and the law professor who recommended that she hire Laura Taylor Swain as her law clerk, that she hired her sight unseen, without even interviewing her.[28] Swain developed a close relationship with Motley, regarding her as a mentor and role model. She paid a tribute to Motley on March 29, 2006, at the Thurgood Marshall Federal Judiciary Building in Washington DC during the celebration of Women's History Month. The tribute included reminiscences about Motley's career as a trial lawyer, a political leader, and a judge.

When Motley was appointed as the first female judge to serve on the District Court for the Southern District of New York, she was also the first black woman to be appointed as a lifetime federal judge in the entire country. As a black woman and a former trial lawyer in a civil rights practice, "she was obviously . . . novel, or at least perceived as novel in her background. Most of the judges on the Southern District had traditionally come out of the prosecutorial arm of the government or out of the major Wall Street law firms," Swain noted. Because Motley was a woman—and especially a black woman—with a legal experiential background that differed from that of most of the men who had been appointed as judges, "there was some skepticism attached to her civil rights background . . . perhaps even more so than many women and people of color perceive today."[29]

There was a presumption by her detractors that Motley might not be up to the task of being a federal judge. She quickly disabused any notions that she was not qualified to perform the job. She developed a reputation as an excellent jurist in all areas of concern in the court, from criminal law to admiralty and securities law, and she certainly held her own on the civil rights front as well.[30]

James Farmer described Motley as having "partly poise and partly supreme self-confidence as a federal judge. If she felt any self-doubt, the law clerks never saw it—she kept it to herself.[31] He also described her as being partly graceful and partly insisting that she be respected as a judge and taken seriously.

Six- and seven-day workweeks and long hours working with her in chambers was the norm. Even so, her law clerks "never saw Motley fazed by workload, court politics, or anything else." Instead, "she always projected a somewhat intimidating level of confidence, presiding knowingly, firmly, and, where appropriate, gently both in and out of the courtroom."[32]

Motley had high expectations for herself, for the management of her chambers and courtroom, and for those who came into her courtroom.[33] The litigants before her always said that she insisted that the lawyers be completely prepared when they presented their cases to her.[34]

In the courtroom Motley was very much the judge and in charge. She was known for the "daunting glare and sharp rebuke" she gave to any lawyer who overstepped his or her bounds during a trial.[35] Motley made it perfectly clear that she was the person presiding and that she was the decision maker of the matters before her.[36] Her law clerks remembered her as being very demanding in many respects and exhibiting an extraordinary toughness.

Farmer recalled that a former prosecutor who appeared regularly in Motley's courtroom commented that from the prosecutors' perspective, she was "a tough law-and-order judge and frequently a tough sentencer, particularly on those who abused their position or had power or advantages and disadvantaged others. She was really intimidating in court. She was God on the bench. . . . Everyone agrees that she could be extraordinarily intimidating," he said.[37]

Although she could be intimidating, Motley was very careful and attentive and went out of her way to make sure that both the lawyers and their clients understood that they were being listened to, that the positions on both sides of a case were being very carefully considered by her, that there was absolute equality in her courtroom, and that ultimately there would be a wise decision by a wise judge.[38]

When he spoke about working in Motley's chambers, Farmer stated that the law clerks were privileged to sit in proximity to her and to share in the very intimate experience of working with her. "This movement lawyer brought to judging the same work habits she had brought to litigation in the South" as a civil rights trial lawyer, he said. [39] Motley worked long hours; she was in the courthouse every morning at 9:00 A.M. and did not leave until 8:30 to 10:00 P.M. most evenings. Farmer and her other law clerks were there with her every day, including Saturdays, during the school year, when she was not going to her country home in Connecticut. They worked in her chambers, "and one of the great rhythms and rituals of the day was spending the evening in the quiet chambers, broken up occasionally by hysterical laughter, until Mr. Motley came to pick her up. Everyone found Mr. Motley their absolute favorite," said Farmer.[40]

Assiduous and *diligent* are terms that were consistently used to describe Motley as a civil rights advocate and a judge. She was obviously very bright, well trained, and an excellent jurist, but what was "underestimated about her was her predacious capacity for plain old hard work driven by the justice of her causes and her commitment to her standards of excellence," Drew Days reported.[41]

Motley's work ethic as a civil rights advocate carried over to her work as a woman and person of color as a judge. "The manner in which she carried forward the habits and the passions of a lifetime in the civil rights war," said Farmer, "were manifested in the manner in which she dealt with the parties before her. . . . It was always a matter of ensuring that everyone received a fair shake" when they appeared before her.[42] To ensure that fairness, Farmer recalled, if a plaintiff brought a case and Motley was convinced that the plaintiff's counsel was not adequately prepared or was incompetent, she would take over and ask most of the questions of the witnesses to ensure that the pertinent factual areas were developed. She was determined that the record would be complete. That was just one of the innumerable ways in which her habits, attitude, and experiences from her role as a lawyer in civil rights battles became part of who she was as a judge.

Motley handled every case conscientiously, for the benefit of the litigants, and with an eye toward doing justice and applying her judicial philosophy that everybody get a "fair shake" in her courtroom. However, Motley was not a sucker for every claim of discrimination brought to her court.[43]

Swain conducted what she characterized as a highly unscientific poll of the eighty law clerks who worked for Motley during the years she served as a judge. The results demonstrated that Motley was consistent in her commitment to justice and clear sense of right and wrong, her high standards, and her ability to remain seemingly aloof while homing in on every detail and rising above any sign of disrespect for her or for her office.[44]

The law clerks' account of the special skills required to work for Motley overlapped substantially. They agreed that accurate lunch procurement was very high on the list, and "woe to the law clerk who got croutons put in the pea soup." The clerks also agreed that the required skills included "fast typing on Selectrics, finding eyeglasses, taking notes on complicated jury instructions, turning around finished products that had Judge Motley convinced [they] could take steno," and always being "ready for field trips" with her to "Cheese of All Nations or to Little Italy," for good meals.[45]

Farmer also conducted unscientific research. The law clerks he communicated with had similar recollections about the attributes Motley displayed. "She demanded respect, . . . she was slightly autocratic, . . . she had dignified honorary grace," and she had an aura that conveyed she was to be taken seriously. The law clerks believed that her imposing demeanor and the way in which she commanded a room when she entered were not acquired as a judge. Rather, they were attributes she brought to the bench with her.[46]

Questions about the treatment male lawyers accorded to Motley as the only woman—and the first black woman—to be a federal court judge were also answered by Farmer. He emphatically stated that she dealt with this by demanding the same respect that lawyers and everyone else involved in the litigation experience extended to the white male judges or any other federal judge.

Farmer recounted an anecdote about a male lawyer who insisted on talking over Motley in her courtroom. "She questioned him and questioned him and questioned him, and finally, when he wouldn't stop [talking over her], she fined him $1,500, found him in contempt [of court], walked out [of the courtroom], and said to her law clerk, 'Men, they always talk over you no matter what you do.'"[47]

It wasn't just the lawyers who appeared before her that Motley demanded respect from, however. She also demanded respect from her law clerks. "She, in ways that we all found very amusing, I think, made perfectly clear who was boss. . . . There was always a sense in which the judge was clear about who was in charge in a way that was terribly endearing," Farmer elaborated. She wasn't saying, "Respect me, Connie Motley, an individual," but "Respect this person of color, this woman, this judge, who deserves to be treated like any other judge in this position."[48]

William Forbath, associate dean and chair in law at the University of Texas Law School and a longtime Motley family friend, also commented on the fact that Motley demanded respect in her courtroom. "After the indignities she had endured from lawyers and judges in the Jim Crow South, she was not going to take grief from any lawyers. It took awhile, and she became notorious for sanctioning lawyers to establish her respect on the bench," he said.[49]

Although Motley was tough and intimidating and demanded respect, she had quite a sense of humor. It was a very wry sense of humor that was not immediately apparent. She was always dignified and usually controlled in her public statements, in her public demeanor, and even in her private chambers. Every now and then she would say or do something surprisingly uncharacteristic that would catch a clerk off guard and make him or her laugh. She was very careful to manage the interaction and situations in which her sense of humor came into play so that it was always appropriate. Swain thought that was part of Motley's success as a communicator, a lawyer, and a judge.[50]

Joel characterized his mother as very formal, dignified, and warm, with a wonderful sense of humor. He told the following anecdote. A few years before her death, Motley received an award from the Federal Bar Council. Before the ceremony she had spent a good deal of time on the phone with the president of the council as he prepared his introduction of her. Later she went to the event, which was held at the Waldorf Astoria "with about a thousand lawyers" in attendance. The president introduced her—a very nice introduction, Joel said. When Motley got up to receive her award, she said, "Mr. Smith, I want to thank you for that lovely introduction." She continued, "And in fact we talked about it on the phone for about an hour, and I had hoped that the conversation would have made the introduction free of errors." Joel said that when his mother made that statement, "you could hear a pin drop. I mean all these litigators, hair standing on their heads; they all wanted to sink under the table." Motley added, "For example, you said I have 31 honorary degrees. I have 33 honorary degrees." At that point "everyone just cracked up. It was a great example of the kind of humor that she had."[51]

Motley had a unique way of making people feel comfortable and encouraging them to engage with her. Swain experienced it and said she always felt encouragement to ask Motley questions and express her thoughts so that she could do her best job as a law clerk. Over the years she heard that other law clerks, especially women, perceived the same sense of welcome and encouragement from Motley, who was proud and protective of all her law clerks.[52]

Swain's fondest memories of Motley were of two social occasions. One occurred during her clerkship year when New York City celebrated the one-hundredth anniversary of the Brooklyn Bridge. From her chambers Motley had a great view of the East River and the Brooklyn Bridge, which had been set up with fireworks. She suggested that the law clerks stay for the evening and watch the celebration from her office. They did, and as the fireworks went off, Judge Motley and her husband stood by the window, where she repeated, "Oooh," "Ahhh," and "That's neat" for the fifteen or twenty minutes of the fireworks show.[53]

The other fond memory Swain had was of the gracious welcome Motley extended to her when Swain was appointed as a district court judge. Motley swore her in. She also hosted a luncheon, invited all the female judges of the Southern and Eastern Districts of New York and the Second Circuit Court of Appeals, and made a very personal introduction of Swain to her new colleagues. That was characteristic of Motley's thoughtfulness, warmth, and care for her former clerks and her friends.[54]

Two weeks before her death from congestive heart failure, Swain and another female judge had an impromptu surprise eighty-fourth birthday celebration for Motley in her chambers. Recalling that event, Swain wrote, "I will treasure the memory of our out-of-tune rendition of happy birthday and her smile and laughter on receiving flowers. . . . I suppose the end [Motley's death while she was still actively serving as a judge] was fitting. She wasn't really ever the retiring type and had remarked to me a few months earlier in an offhand way . . .

that she really had no idea what she'd do if she weren't working on cases and coming into chambers regularly."[55]

Motley's commitment to hard work and excellence was apparent throughout her nearly four decades of service as a federal judge, in which she decided twenty-five hundred cases. The range of her rulings was broad and extensive. She issued what may have been her most controversial ruling in *Sostre v. Rockefeller*, a prisoner's rights (due process) case brought by Martin Sostre, a black prisoner who was very active in bringing lawsuits against New York State prison officials.[56] He had been punished and put in solitary confinement for doing things like writing a letter to his sister, having law review articles in his cell, and "other ridiculous things like that," Motley said. Sostre claimed that he had been brutally mistreated by being put into solitary.[57]

The question before Motley was this: What due process rights do prisoners have? During the trial, psychiatrists and psychologists testified that solitary confinement for more than two weeks was mentally harmful to a person. Sostre had been kept in solitary for more than a year. Motley ruled that such a long period of solitary confinement constituted cruel and unusual punishment and was a violation of the Eighth Amendment. She awarded the plaintiff monetary damages against the state of New York. The Second Circuit Court of Appeals reversed the award of damages to Sostre, but it did affirm Motley's ruling that he had been punished for things that were not really crimes and that it was a violation of his due process rights to put him in solitary confinement for such things.[58]

The case received extensive publicity. Motley was heavily criticized for her decision protecting prisoners' rights. Some argued that she had overstepped her authority as a judge and had inserted her background as a civil rights advocate in the case. She rejected the criticism and expressed her view that when it comes to protecting rights, somebody had to have the courage to start doing it and be willing to be criticized for doing what was right, fair, and just. She believed that the *Sostre* case was one of the early decisions about prisoners' rights and that it "started the whole process of trying to establish what rights prisoners have." She also believed that the "real" issue concerning her ruling in favor of Sostre was whether she had gone too far and too fast in protecting prisoners' rights. Motley analogized her decision in the case to her experience in the South during the civil rights movement. "Well, you know the history of the whole civil rights movement. . . . Every time we [the LDF] brought a case we were always going too fast, weren't we? That was always one of the things we were criticized for. But you have to start somewhere" to achieve fairness and justice, she said.[59]

Motley also protected the right of gay protesters to picket the Catholic Church's stance on homosexuality in front of St. Patrick's Cathedral as the Gay Pride Parade passed by. The protesters alleged that their civil rights had been violated when they were refused permission to assemble on the public sidewalk in front of the church, and Motley ruled in their favor. When questioned about her ruling, she replied, "I said they could march [in front of St. Patrick's Cathedral] because the sidewalk is owned by the city, not the Church."[60]

Motley was a trailblazer who broke through the gender gap to become the first female lawyer at the LDF, the only female trial lawyer in courts in the South during most of the civil rights movement, the first woman elected to major political offices in New York, and the first female federal court judge. With the accomplishment of so many impressive firsts, Motley would seem to be a black feminist. But she did not consider herself to be a feminist at all. On several occasions she bluntly declared, "I'm not a feminist." Yet even though she wasn't a feminist in the sense of being an activist in the women's liberation movement, she was fierce in the protection of women as well as other plaintiffs in discrimination cases in her court.[61]

In *Letke v. Bouie Kuhn*, for example, a female sports reporter challenged the policy that permitted male sports reporters to enter male locker rooms after games to interview players but excluded female reporters from doing so. Motley had to rule on the issue of whether female sports reporters should be allowed access to the Yankees' locker room to conduct interviews at Yankee Stadium during the World Series so that they could perform their jobs without restriction in the same way that male reporters did. Motley was not deterred by the defense argument that female reporters would have to be in a locker room filled with men, many of whom were naked and showering after their game. "They [the players] can wear towels" and cover up, Motley said, ruling in favor of the plaintiff.[62] Her decision was important for women's employment rights.

In her prior career as a civil rights lawyer, Motley had not been an advocate for issues that concerned women exclusively. She had not joined or actively supported feminist organizations, activities, or ideology. She had not become actively engaged in the women's rights movement. She had primarily been an advocate for social change and a leader in helping to uplift the black race and the black community. She had used her intellect, influence, and power within the legal system and the courts as venues for her battle against racial inequality and segregation in American society.

By the time the feminist movement fully developed, Motley was no longer an advocate or civil rights activist; she had become a federal judge. As a judge, she was required to interpret and apply the law, not to actively work to change it. Even if she had not become a judge, she probably would not have been involved in the feminist movement. She wrote as follows about her relationship with the feminist movement:

> Although I was the first black woman in the New York State Senate, the first woman Manhattan borough president, and the first woman on

the federal bench in New York, I had no particular attachment to the newest women's rights movement, which emerged about 1965, the year I became borough president. I remember meeting with Betty Friedan before she wrote *The Feminine Mystique*. Our children attended the same grammar school, Dalton, and we had been mommies together, exchanging home visits and such.

In my view, I did not get to the federal bench because I was a woman. I understood my appointment as based on my accomplishments as a civil rights lawyer.[63]

Motley "distinguished herself in all different areas of the law . . . and proved that a woman was . . . the equal of anyone else who was qualified to serve on the court," said Swain. She "ultimately led the court with distinction as well. . . . She was a giant in the federal judiciary."[64]

In 1982, Motley accomplished another first when she became the first woman to serve as the chief justice of the District Court for the Southern District of New York. In 1986 she assumed senior status, a position she held until her death on September 28, 2005.

Motley "certainly did not promote herself or . . . toot her horn," said John Brittain, a law school professor and former General Counsel for the Lawyers Committee for Civil Rights and Motley family friend. Yet the extraordinary work she performed and the cases she won during the civil rights movement speak for themselves.[65] She may have been marginalized by historians who wrote male-centered narratives of the movement and overlooked by the white mainstream media that covered the movement; however, the black media highlighted her victories that helped eradicate Jim Crow. In addition, thirty-three colleges and universities awarded her honorary degrees for outstanding achievement as a trailblazer who knocked down barriers as a civil rights lawyer and an agent of change.

Motley also received hundreds of awards and citations from professional, social, and civil rights organizations. The national NAACP presented her with the Spingarn Medal, its highest honor and award. In 2001 President Bill Clinton awarded her the Presidential Citizens Medal in recognition of her many years of extraordinary service. He observed, "As a dedicated public servant and distinguished judge," Motley had "broken down political, social, and professional barriers, and her pursuit of equal justice under the law widened the circle of opportunity in America."[66]

Although Motley declined the opportunity to have the federal court building at 500 Pearl Street named in her honor, she agreed to have the jury assembly room renamed the Constance Baker Motley Jury Assembly Room in 2002. Her former law clerks donated a stunning portrait of her to be hung there.[67] Noting that Motley had "had the opportunity to have the entire courthouse named for her" but had declined, Swain shared the remarks of the court's chief justice at Motley's memorial service:

As many of you know, we named the Jury Assembly Room for Judge Motley, and when I went to her chambers to tell her the good news, she was quite pleased, of course, but she took the occasion to show me a copy of a note Senator [Daniel] Moynihan sent her suggesting that this building should be named after her. Characteristically, she declined that honor, and, of course, we all know the building eventually came to be named after Senator Moynihan. But she did let it be known in her own good and subtle way, even as I delivered the cheerful news about the naming of the Jury Room, that she could have had the whole thing.[68]

Conclusion

This book has centered on Constance Baker Motley and the work she performed as a civil rights movement lawyer. It has focused on her victories in the courtroom that affected the strategies and outcomes of the civil rights movement, accelerated the end of Jim Crow segregation, led to equality in many aspects of life for blacks and whites, and made major long-term changes that helped transform the United States into a more inclusive, equal, just, and democratic society.

Motley exhibited a leadership style that reflected her personality traits, skills, and strengths. She was a visionary who devised and implemented the legal strategy for the NAACP's civil rights cases. She formed alliances and inspired local lawyers to work with her to achieve the goals of the civil rights movement. As a leader and an agent of change, Motley was committed to the cause of justice. She devoted her attention and energy to the task at hand and was not easily distracted. She directed those who worked with her on what to do and how to do it to achieve the desired result. She did not hold the title of director counsel—the formal leader—of the LDF; however, she performed important work in the trenches in the South and behind the scenes in courts that helped make the civil rights movement successful.

Motley was an excellent orator and a formidable trial lawyer who was tough, independent, formal, reserved, decisive, courageous, and not afraid to make hard decisions or venture into dangerous situations. These are just a few of the many attributes she exhibited during her career at the LDF. She responded quickly to crisis situations when immediate action was required. She was persistent, persuasive, strong, confident, patient, and compassionate but not warm and fuzzy.

Protest action was an important strategy in the civil rights movement. Legal victories were also important in achieving significant social and political change. Motley's work in the courts was crucial in securing those gains. For close to twenty years she was a key strategist and trial lawyer who fought to implement the Supreme Court's ruling in *Brown v. Board of Education* and desegregate America. She worked incessantly and won some of the most significant desegregation cases; she championed the cause of equal rights and advanced the goals of the civil rights movement.

During the civil rights movement, racial barriers were torn down so that blacks as well as whites could freely move and participate in the larger society. "The cases that Constance Baker Motley won . . . helped to put the nails in the coffin of legalized inequality in America," said Lynn Huntley, a noted civil rights advocate and former LDF staff attorney. "They vindicated the rights of ordinary black people to be affirmed by their fellow Americans and agencies of government as equal, sentient, and valued human beings whose rights deserve vindication and protection.[1]

Motley's victories opened doors that had previously been closed to blacks. As a result of her action and agency, blacks no longer had to confine themselves to public facilities designated "colored only." They were no longer excluded from public accommodations or institutions that were designated "white only."

With the assistance of her colleagues at the LDF and local lawyers, Motley won cases that protected the right of blacks to register and vote; attend desegregated public schools, colleges, and universities; ride and sit in any empty seat on interstate buses and trains; sit in waiting rooms and use bathroom facilities in bus terminals and train stations; be served and eat at lunch counters and restaurants; go to parks, museums, and other places of public recreation; and stay in hotels on an equal basis with whites. The victories in the courts dismantled a whole way of life—a segregated society. They forced two presidents—the executive branch of the federal government—to take action, federalize troops, and send these troops to end the violence that erupted when blacks attempted to enter all-white schools and desegregate them. They also provided the necessary impetus to force Congress—the legislative branch of the federal government—to enact laws (civil rights acts) to dismantle legal segregation in the nation.

The victories in the cases that desegregated public schools, colleges, universities, and professional schools made it possible for blacks to become well educated, obtain better jobs, and move up economically. They expanded the black middle class and made it possible for blacks to move into careers and employment in major governmental positions, corporations, and other areas that had previously not been available to them solely because of their race.

The victories in the cases that protected the right of blacks to register and vote facilitated the development of black political power and the election of black mayors, governors, members of Congress, and local and state officials throughout the country; they provided blacks access to the political power structure. They empowered the black masses to become politically active and able to force state legislatures and Congress to appropriate money for education, roads, and housing in black communities and to represent the interests of their black constituents in the same way that they protected their white constituents.

As a result of Jim Crow laws and the vestiges of slavery, blacks suffered psychological damage, felt inferior to whites, and were powerless in society. In *Brown* the LDF argued that state-mandated public school segregation affected the ability of black children to learn because they saw themselves as inferior people and this became a self-fulfilling prophecy.

"One of the effects of segregation was to make blacks feel inferior," said Motley, "because the reality for them was that they were inferior in the society, that the white people were the privileged people, and they were underprivileged people. Every black child could see that blacks had less than whites, and therefore black children grew up feeling that they were in fact inferior." Motley believed that the inferiority attitude manifested itself in efforts by the NAACP to get blacks to participate in desegregation cases. "They were fearful; they knew that the white community was powerful," she stated. "They felt there was no hope; they felt that black people just could not overcome this powerful" system of racial segregation. They felt powerless.[2] As a result of court victories that ended legal segregation and provided equality and inclusion for blacks, they no longer felt inferior or powerless. They developed self-esteem, self-assurance, and pride in their heritage and culture. Black communities as well as individuals became empowered.

The work that Motley and other LDF lawyers and local counsel performed also benefited whites. Jim Crow laws that had prohibited blacks from sitting in white-only areas on buses or in restaurants or from using white-only restrooms had also prohibited whites from entering or using black-only facilities. Victory in the desegregation cases opened all public institutions, facilities, and accommodations to both blacks and whites on an equal basis and without regard to race.

Through her agency in the courts, Motley helped break down political, social, and professional barriers. Her tireless pursuit of equal justice under the law widened the circle of opportunity for blacks, whites, women, and the other groups that were discriminated against and denied equality in American society. Her actions as a trailblazer in the legal profession created opportunities for women—both black and white—to work as business lawyers, law professors and deans, legal services lawyers, partners in law firms, corporate officers, judges, governmental lawyers, and executives in nonprofit and for-profit business entities. She also paved the way and served as a role model for women to work as political leaders and in all other positions formerly held only by men.

Constance Baker Motley's agency and actions provide persuasive evidence that formal male activism should no longer be viewed as the only style of leader-ship that was effective or acceptable during the civil rights movement. Her actions also provide persuasive evidence that traditional historical narratives of the civil rights movement should be revised to fully examine her life and contributions, to write her into the narratives, and to write in other diverse female activists and change agents who performed their work in many different venues and political spaces and who utilized alternative styles of leadership during the movement.

Appendix
Constance Baker Motley's NAACP Legal Defense and Educational Fund Cases

United States Supreme Court

Swain v. Alabama, 380 U.S. 202, 85 S. Ct. 824, 13 L. Ed. 2d 759 (1965). Peremptory challenges to exclude blacks from petit jury.

Blow v. North Carolina, 379 U.S. 684, 85 S. Ct. 635, 13 L. Ed. 2d 603 (1965). Restaurant, trespass prosecution.

Hamm v. City of Rock Hill, Lupper v. State of Arkansas, 379 U.S. 306, 85 S. Ct. 384, 13 L. Ed. 2d 300 (1964). Lunch-counter sit-ins, trespass prosecution; South Carolina, Arkansas.

Barr v. City of Columbia, 378 U.S. 146, 84 S. Ct. 1734, 12 L. Ed. 2d 766 (1964). Lunch-counter sit-ins, trespass prosecution; South Carolina.

Bouie v. City of Columbia, 378 U.S. 347, 84 S. Ct. 1697, 12 L. Ed. 2d 894 (1964). Lunch-counter sit-ins, trespass prosecution; South Carolina.

Calhoun v. Latimer, 377 U.S. 263, 84 S. Ct. 1235, 12 L. Ed. 2d 288 (1964). Atlanta school desegregation; Georgia.

Katzenbach v. McClung, 379 U.S. 802, 85 S. Ct. 11, 13 L. Ed. 2d 20 (1964). Public accommodations, restaurant, constitutionality of Civil Rights Act of 1964 as applied to restaurant and interstate travel; Alabama.

Mitchell v. City of Charleston, 378 U.S. 551, 84 S. Ct. 1901, 12 L. Ed. 2d 1033 (1964). Lunch-counter sit-ins, trespass prosecution; South Carolina.

Hamm v. City of Rock Hill, 377 U.S. 988, 84 S. Ct. 1902, 12 L. Ed. 2d 1042 (1964). Lunch-counter sit-ins, trespass prosecution; South Carolina.

Lupper v. Arkansas, 377 U.S. 989, 84 S. Ct. 1906, 12 L. Ed. 2d 1043 (1964). Lunch-counter sit-ins, trespass prosecution.

Swain v. Alabama, 377 U.S. 915, 84 S. Ct. 1183, 12 L. Ed. 2d 185 (1964). Peremptory challenges to exclude blacks from petit jury.

Henry v. City of Rock Hill, 376 U.S. 776, 84 S. Ct. 1042, 12 L. Ed. 2d 79 (1964). Breach-of-peace prosecution; South Carolina.

Gibson v. Harris, 376 U.S. 908, 84 S. Ct. 661, 11 L. Ed. 2d 606 (1964). School desegregation; Georgia, Alabama.

City of Jackson v. Bailey, 376 U.S. 910, 84 S. Ct. 666, 11 L. Ed. 2d 609 (1964). Desegregation, transportation, common carriers; Mississippi.

Calhoun v. Latimer, 375 U.S. 983, 84 S. Ct. 516, 11 L. Ed. 2d 472 (1964). Atlanta school desegregation; Georgia.

Abernathy v. Alabama, 375 U.S. 963, 84 S. Ct. 485, 11 L. Ed. 2d 413 (1964). Desegregation, interstate transportation facilities, trespass prosecution.

Watson v. City of Memphis, 373 U.S. 526, 83 S. Ct. 1314, 10 L. Ed. 2d 529 (1963). Desegregation, public parks, recreational facilities; Tennessee.

Shuttlesworth v. City of Birmingham, 373 U.S. 262, 83 S. Ct. 1130, 10 L. Ed. 2d 335 (1963). Lunch-counter sit-ins, trespass prosecution; Alabama.

Gober v. City of Birmingham, 373 U.S. 374, 83 S. Ct. 1311, 10 L. Ed. 2d 419 (1963). Lunch-counter sit-ins, trespass prosecution; Alabama.

Fields v. South Carolina, 375 U.S. 44, 84 S. Ct. 149, 11 L. Ed. 2d 107 (1963). Breach-of-peace prosecution.

Henry v. City of Rock Hill, 375 U.S. 6, 84 S. Ct. 44, 11 L. Ed. 2d 38 (1963). Breach-of-peace prosecution; South Carolina.

Thompson v. Virginia, 374 U.S. 99, 83 S. Ct. 1686, 10 L. Ed. 2d 1025 (1963). Lunch-counter sit-ins, trespass prosecution.

Bouie v. City of Columbia, 374 U.S. 805, 83 S. Ct. 1690, 10 L. Ed. 2d 1030 (1963). Lunch-counter sit-ins, trespass prosecution; South Carolina.

Bell v. Maryland, 374 U.S. 805, 83 S. Ct. 1691, 10 L. Ed. 2d 1030 (1963). Lunch-counter sit-ins, trespass prosecution.

Fields v. South Carolina, 372 U.S. 522, 83 S. Ct. 887, 9 L. Ed. 2d 965 (1963). Breach-of peace prosecution.

Turner v. City of Memphis, 369 U.S. 350, 82 S. Ct. 805, 7 L. Ed. 2d 762 (1962). Desegregation, transportation, municipal airport restaurant; Tennessee.

Watson v. City of Memphis, 371 U.S. 909, 83 S. Ct. 256, 9 L. Ed. 2d 169 (1962). Desegregation, public parks, recreational facilities; Tennessee.

Shuttlesworth v. City of Birmingham, 370 U.S. 934, 82 S. Ct. 1580, 8 L. Ed. 2d 805 (1962). Lunch-counter sit-ins, trespass prosecution; Alabama.

Gober v. City of Birmingham, 370 U.S. 934, 82 S. Ct. 1580, 8 L. Ed. 2d 805 (1962). Lunch-counter sit-ins, trespass prosecutions; Alabama.

Wright v. State of Georgia, 370 U.S. 935, 82 S. Ct. 1580, 8 L. Ed. 2d 806 (1962). Breach-of-peace prosecution.

Peterson v. City of Greenville, 370 U.S. 935, 82 S. Ct. 1577, 8 L. Ed. 2d 806 (1962). Lunch-counter sit-ins, trespass prosecution; South Carolina.

Northcross v. Board of Education of City of Memphis, 370 U.S. 944, 82 S. Ct. 1586, 8 L. Ed. 2d 810 (1962). School desegregation; Tennessee.

Edwards v. South Carolina, 369 U.S. 870, 82 S. Ct. 1141, 8 L. Ed. 2d 274 (1962). Breach-of-peace prosecution.

Bailey v. Patterson, 369 U.S. 31, 82 S. Ct. 549, 7 L. Ed. 2d 512 (1962). Desegregation, interstate and intrastate transportation; Mississippi.

Bailey v. Patterson, 368 U.S. 963, 82 S. Ct. 440 (1962). Desegregation, interstate and intrastate transportation; Mississippi.

Hamilton v. State of Alabama, 368 U.S. 52, 82 S. Ct. 157, 7 L. Ed. 2d 114 (1961). Right to counsel at arraignment, capital case.

Bailey v. Patterson, 368 U.S. 346, 82 S. Ct. 282, 7 L. Ed. 2d 332 (1961). Desegregation, interstate and intrastate transportation; Mississippi.

Board of Education of City School District of City of New Rochelle v. Taylor, 368 U.S. 940, 82 S. Ct. 382, 7 L. Ed. 2d 339 (1961). School desegregation; New York.

Turner v. City of Memphis, 368 U.S. 808, 82 S. Ct. 31, 7 L. Ed. 2d 19 (1961). Desegregation, transportation, municipal airport restaurant; Tennessee.

Louisiana State Board of Education v. Allen, 368 U.S. 830, 82 S. Ct. 52, 7 L. Ed. 2d 33 (1961). Trade school desegregation.

St. Helena Parish School Board v. Hall, 368 U.S. 830, 82 S. Ct. 52, 7 L. Ed. 2d 33 (1961). School desegregation; Louisiana.

Kennard v. Mississippi, 368 U.S. 869, 82 S. Ct. 111, 7 L. Ed. 2d 66 (1961). Exclusion of blacks from grand and petit juries.

Danner v. Holmes, 364 U.S. 939, 81 S. Ct. 686 (1961). University of Georgia desegregation.

Harrison v. National Association for the Advancement of Colored People, 360 U.S. 167, 79 S. Ct. 1025 (1960). School desegregation, registry and barratry statutes; Virginia.

United States v. Louisiana, Bush v. Orleans Parish School Board, Williams v. Davis, 364 U.S. 500, 81 S. Ct. 260, 5 L. Ed. 2d 245 (1960). School desegregation.

Bush v. Orleans Parish School Board, 364 U.S. 803, 81 S. Ct. 28, 5 L. Ed. 2d 36 (1960). School desegregation; Louisiana.

Davis v. Williams, 364 U.S. 803, 81 S. Ct. 28, 5 L. Ed. 2d 36 (1960). School desegregation; Louisiana.

Orleans Parish School Board v. Bush, 364 U.S. 803, 81 S. Ct. 28, 5 L. Ed. 2d 36 (1960). School desegregation; Louisiana.

Boynton v. Virginia, 361 U.S. 958, 80 S. Ct. 584, 4 L. Ed. 2d 541 (1960). Desegregation, interstate transportation facilities, terminal restaurant.

Kelley v. Board of Education of City of Nashville, Davidson County, Tennessee, 361 U.S. 924, 80 S. Ct. 293, 4 L. Ed. 2d 240 (1959). School desegregation.

Cohen v. Public Housing Administration, 358 U.S. 928, 79 S. Ct. 315, 3 L. Ed. 2d 302 (1959). Savannah housing desegregation; Georgia.

Harrison v. National Association for the Advancement of Colored People, 358 U.S. 807, 79 S. Ct. 33, 3 L. Ed. 2d 53 (1958). School desegregation, registration and barratry statutes; Virginia.

Aaron v. Cooper, 357 U.S. 566, 78 S. Ct. 1189, 2 L. Ed. 2d 1544 (1958). Little Rock school desegregation; Arkansas.

Speed v. City of Tallahassee, Florida, 356 U.S. 913, 78 S. Ct. 670, 2 L. Ed. 2d 586 (1958). School desegregation.

Adams v. Lucy, 351 U.S. 931, 76 S. Ct. 790, 100 L. Ed. 2d 1460 (1956). University of Alabama desegregation.

Board of Education of Hillsboro, Ohio v. Clemons, 350 U.S. 1006, 76 S. Ct. 651, 100 L. Ed. 868 (1956). School desegregation.

Lucy v. Adams, 350 U.S. 1, 76 S. Ct. 33, 100 L. Ed. 2d 3 (1955). School desegregation.

Brown v. Board of Education of Topeka, Kansas, 347 U.S. 483, 74 S. Ct. 686, 98 L. Ed. 2d 873 (1954), supp. by 349 U.S. 294, 75 S. Ct. 753, 99 L. Ed. 1083 (1955). School desegregation.

United States Courts of Appeals Cases

Rabinowitz v. United States, Jackson v. United States, 366 F.2d 34 (5th Cir. 1966). Exclusion of blacks from jury list, federal prosecution for perjury; Georgia.

Singleton v. Board of Com'rs of State Institutions, 356 F.2d 771 (5th Cir. 1966). Reform school desegregation; Florida.

Jackson Municipal Separate School District v. Evers, 357 F.2d 653 (5th Cir. 1966). School desegregation; Mississippi.

Henry v. Coahoma County Bd. of Ed., 353 F.2d 648 (5th Cir. 1965). Employment, fired teacher, member of NAACP; Mississippi.

Hammond v. University of Tampa, 344 F.2d 951 (5th Cir. 1965). University desegregation.

Flagler Hospital, Inc. v. Hayling, 344 F.2d 950 (5th Cir. 1965). Desegregation, hospital facilities, dining rooms, bathrooms; Florida.

United States v. Barnett, 346 F.2d 99 (5th Cir. 1965). University of Mississippi desegregation, contempt.

Morrison Cafeteria Co. of Nashville, Inc. v. Johnson, 344 F.2d 690 (6th Cir. 1965). Demonstrations, attempt by cafeteria owner to enjoin; Tennessee.

Lockett v. Board of Ed. of Muscogee County School Dist., Ga., 342 F.2d 225 (5th Cir. 1965). Columbus school desegregation.

Bivins v. Board of Public Ed. and Orphanage for Bibb County, Ga., 342 F.2d 229 (5th Cir. 1965). School desegregation.

Wimbish v. Pinellas County, Fla., 342 F.2d 804 (5th Cir. 1965). Desegregation, public recreational facilities, golf course.

Smith v. Holiday Inns of America, Inc., 336 F.2d 630 (6th Cir. 1964). Motel desegregation; Tennessee.

Gaines v. Dougherty County Bd. of Ed., 334 F.2d 983 (5th Cir. 1964). School desegregation; Georgia.

Zellner v. Lingo, 334 F.2d 620 (5th Cir. 1964). Demonstrations, Civil Rights Act, criminal prosecutions, freedom walkers; Alabama.

Woods v. Wright, 334 F.2d 369 (5th Cir 1964). Birmingham demonstrations, expelled schoolchildren; Alabama.

Kelly v. Page, 335 F.2d 114 (5th Cir. 1964). Desegregation, Albany public facilities; Georgia.

Armstrong v. Board of Ed. of City of Birmingham, Jefferson County, Alabama, 333 F.2d 47 (5th Cir. 1964). School desegregation.

Davis v. Board of School Commissioner of Mobile County, Alabama, 333 F.2d 53 (5th Cir. 1964). School desegregation.

Stell v. Savannah-Chatham County Bd. of Ed., 333 F.2d 55 (5th Cir. 1964). School desegregation; Georgia.

Northcross v. Board of Ed. of City of Memphis, 333 F.2d 661 (6th Cir. 1964). School desegregation; Tennessee.

Parker v. Franklin, 331 F.2d 841 (5th Cir. 1964). University of Alabama graduate school desegregation.

Eaton v. Grubbs, 329 F.2d 710 (4th Cir. 1964). Desegregation, public facilities, hospital; North Carolina.

Gaines v. Dougherty County Bd. of Ed., 329 F. 2d 823 (5th Cir. 1964). Albany school desegregation; Georgia.

McCorvey v. Lucy, 328 F.2d 892 (5th Cir. 1964). University of Alabama desegregation.

Evers v. Jackson Municipal Separate School District, 328 F.2d 408 (5th Cir. 1964). School desegregation; Mississippi.

Brown v. School District No. 20, Charleston, South Carolina, 328 F.2d 618 (4th Cir. 1964). School desegregation.

Board of Public Instruction of Duval County, Florida v. Braxton, 326 F.2d 616 (5th Cir. 1964). Jacksonville school desegregation.

Bailey v. Patterson, 323 F.2d 201 (5th Cir. 1963). Desegregation, interstate and intrastate transportation; Mississippi.

Harris v. Gibson, 322 F.2d 780 (5th Cir. 1963). Brunswick school desegregation; Georgia.

Anderson v. City of Albany, 321 F.2d 649 (5th Cir. 1963). Desegregation, public facilities; Georgia.

Armstrong v. Board of Education of City of Birmingham, Jefferson County, Alabama, 323 F.2d 333 (5th Cir. 1963). School desegregation.

Davis v. Board of School Com'rs of Mobile County, Alabama, 322 F.2d 356 (5th Cir. 1963). School desegregation.

Mapp v. Board of Ed. of City of Chattanooga, Tenn., 319 F.2d 571 (6th Cir. 1963). School desegregation.

Calhoun v. Latimer, 321 F.2d 302 (5th Cir. 1963). Atlanta school desegregation; Georgia.

Davis v. Board of School Com'rs of Mobile County, Alabama, 318 F.2d 63 (5th Cir. 1963). School desegregation.

Stell v. Savannah-Chatham County Bd. of Ed., 318 F.2d 425 (5th Cir. 1963). School desegregation; Georgia.

United States v. Barnett, 316 F.2d 236 (5th Cir. 1963). University of Mississippi desegregation, contempt.

Gantt v. Clemson Agr. College of S.C., 320 F.2d 611 (4th Cir. 1963). University desegregation.

Stone v. Members of Bd. of Ed. of the City of Atlanta, Georgia, 309 F.2d 638 (5th Cir. 1962). School desegregation.

Meredith v. Fair, 328 F.2d 586 (5th Cir. 1962). University of Mississippi desegregation, contempt.

Meredith v. Fair, 313 F.2d 534 (5th Cir. 1962). University of Mississippi desegregation, contempt.

Meredith v. Fair, 313 F.2d 532 (5th Cir. 1962). University of Mississippi desegregation, contempt.

Nelson v. Grooms, 307 F.2d 76 (5th Cir. 1962). Birmingham school desegregation; Alabama.

Bush v. Orleans Parish School Bd., 308 F.2d 491 (5th Cir. 1962). New Orleans school desegregation; Louisiana.

Meredith v. Fair, 306 F.2d 374 (5th Cir. 1962). University of Mississippi desegregation.

Augustus v. Board of Public Instruction of Escambia County, Florida, 306 F.2d 862 (5th Cir. 1962). Pensacola school desegregation.

Meredith v. Fair, 305 F.2d 343 (5th Cir. 1962). University of Mississippi desegregation.

Watson v. City of Memphis, 303 F.2d 863 (6th Cir. 1962). Desegregation, parks, recreational facilities.

Hampton v. City of Jacksonville, Florida, 304 F.2d 320 (5th Cir. 1962). Desegregation, public recreational facilities, golf course.

Christian v. Jemison, 303 F.2d 52 (5th Cir. 1962). Desegregation, Baton Rouge transportation companies; Louisiana.

Turner v. City of Memphis, 301 F.2d 310 (6th Cir. 1962). Desegregation, transportation, municipal airport restaurant; Tennesseee.

Northcross v. Board of Ed. of City of Memphis, Tenn., 302 F.2d 818 (6th Cir. 1962). School desegregation.

Stoudenmire v. Braxton, 299 F.2d 846 (5th Cir. 1962). Duval County school desegregation;, Florida.

Meredith v. Fair, 305 F.2d 341 (5th Cir. 1962). University of Mississippi desegregation.

Meredith v. Fair, 298 F.2d 696 (5th Cir. 1962). University of Mississippi desegregation.

Mapp v. Board of Ed. of City of Chattanooga, Hamilton County, Tenn., 295 F.2d 617 (6th Cir. 1961). School desegregation.

Taylor v. Board of Ed. of City School Dist. of City of New Rochelle, 294 F.2d 36 (2d Cir. 1961). School desegregation; New York.

Taylor v. Board of Ed. of City School Dist. of City of New Rochelle, 288 F.2d 600 (2d Cir. 1961). School desegregation; New York.

Louisiana State Board of Education v. Allen, 287 F.2d 32 (5th Cir. 1961). Trade school desegregation.

Louisiana State Board of Education v. Angel, 287 F.2d 33 (5th Cir. 1961). Trade school desegregation.

East Baton Rouge Parish School Board v. Davis, 287 F.2d 380 (5th Cir. 1961). School desegregation; Louisiana.

Mannings v. Board of Public Instruction of Hillsborough County, Florida, 277 F.2d 370 (5th Cir. 1960). School desegregation.

Tonkins v. City of Greensboro, North Carolina, 276 F.2d 890 (4th Cir. 1960). Desegregation, public swimming pool.

Boson v. Rippy, 275 F.2d 850 (5th Cir. 1960). Dallas school desegregation; Texas.

Orleans Parish School Board v. Bush, 268 F.2d 78 (5th Cir. 1959). New Orleans school desegregation; Louisiana.

Prater v. Boyd, 263 F.2d 788 (6th Cir. 1959). Memphis State University desegregation; Tennessee.

Aaron v. Cooper, 261 F.2d 97 (8th Cir. 1958). Little Rock school desegregation; Arkansas.

Aaron v. Cooper, 257 F.2d 33 (8th Cir. 1958). Little Rock school desegregation; Arkansas.

Cohen v. Public Housing Administration, 257 F.2d 73 (5th Cir. 1958). Savannah housing desegregation; Georgia.

Hawkins v. Board of Control of Florida, 253 F.2d 752 (5th Cir. 1958). University of Florida desegregation.

Gibson v. Board of Public Instruction of Dade County, Florida, 246 F.2d 913 (5th Cir. 1957). School desegregation.

Heyward v. Public Housing Administration, 238 F.2d 689 (5th Cir. 1956). Savannah housing desegregation; Georgia.

Clemons v. Board of Ed. of Hillsboro, Ohio, 228 F.2d 853 (6th Cir. 1956). School desegregation.

Adams v. Lucy, 228 F.2d 619 (5th Cir. 1955). University of Alabama desegregation.

Lucy v. Adams, 228 F.2d 620 (5th Cir. 1955). University of Alabama desegregation.

Detroit Housing Commission v. Lewis, 226 F.2d 180 (6th Cir. 1955). Housing desegregation.

Ex parte Clemons, 218 F.2d 956 (6th Cir. 1954). Hillsboro school desegregation; Ohio.

Lucy v. Board of Trustees of University of Alabama, 213 F.2d 846 (5th Cir. 1954). University of Alabama desegregation.

Heyward v. Public Housing Administration, 214 F.2d 222 (D.C. Cir. 1954). Savannah housing desegregation; Georgia.

Davis v. Arn, 199 F.2d 424 (5th Cir. 1952). Employment discrimination, Mobile County police and fire exams; Alabama.

Bates v. Batte, 187 F.2d 142 (5th Cir. 1951). Employment, equal pay, Jackson teachers' salaries;, Mississippi.

Baskin v. Brown, 174 F.2d 391 (4th Cir. 1949). White Democratic Party primaries; South Carolina.

Rice v. Elmore, 165 F.2d 387 (4th Cir. 1947). Discrimination in Democratic primary election; South Carolina.

Federal District Court Cases

Monroe v. Board of Ed., Madison County, Tenn., 269 F. Supp. 758 (W.D. Tenn. 1965). School desegregation.

Monroe v. Board of Com'rs, City of Jackson, Tenn., 244 F. Supp. 353 (W.D. Tenn. 1965). School desegregation.

Willis v. Pickrick Restaurant, 234 F. Supp. 179 (N.D. Ga. 1964). Desegregation, Atlanta public accommodations, restaurant, constitutionality of Civil Rights Act of 1964.

Willis v. Pickrick Restaurant, 231 F. Supp. 396 (N.D. Ga. 1964). Desegregation, Atlanta public accommodations, restaurant, constitutionality of Civil Rights Act of 1964.

Lee v. Macon County Bd. of Ed., 231 F. Supp. 743 (M.D. Ala. 1964). School desegregation.

Farmer v. Moses, 232 F. Supp. 154 (S.D.N.Y. 1964). Demonstrations, picketing, distributing handbills at World's Fair.

Youngblood v. Board of Public Instruction of Bay County, Fla., 230 F. Supp. 74 (N.D. Fla. 1964). School desegregation.

Franklin v. Parker, 223 F. Supp. 724 (M.D. Ala. 1963). University of Alabama graduate school desegregation.

Lee v. Macon County Bd. of Ed., 221 F. Supp. 297 (M.D. Ala. 1963). School desegregation.

Brown v. School District No. 20, Charleston, South Carolina, 226 F. Supp. 819 (E.D.S.C. 1963). School desegregation.

Monroe v. Board of Com'rs of City of Jackson, Tenn., 221 F. Supp. 968 (W.D. Tenn. 1963). School desegregation.

Smith v. Holiday Inns of America, Inc., 220 F. Supp. 1 (M.D. Tenn. 1963). Motel desegregation.

Davis v. East Baton Rouge Parish School Bd., 219 F. Supp. 876 (E.D. La. 1963). School desegregation.

Gaines v. Dougherty County Bd. of Ed., 222 F. Supp. 166 (M.D. Ga. 1963). School desegregation.

Stell v. Savannah-Chatham County Bd. of Ed., 220 F. Supp. 667 (S.D. Ga. 1963). School desegregation.

Davis v. Board of School Com'rs of Mobile County, Ala., 219 F. Supp. 542 (S.D. Ala. 1963). School desegregation.

Zellner v. Lingo, 218 F. Supp. 513 (M.D. Ala. 1963). Demonstrations, Civil Rights Act, criminal prosecutions, freedom walkers.

Lucy v. Adams, 224 F. Supp. 79 (N.D. Ala. 1963). University of Alabama desegregation.

Davis v. East Baton Rouge Parish School Bd., 214 F. Supp. 624 (E.D. La. 1963). School desegregation.

Anderson v. Kelly, 32 F.R.D. 355 (M.D. Ga. 1963). Desegregation, Albany public facilities.

Gantt v. Clemson Agr. College of South Carolina, 213 F. Supp. 103 (W.D.S.C. 1962). College desegregation.

Calhoun v. Latimer, 217 F. Supp. 614 (N.D. Ga. 1962). Atlanta school desegregation.

Gantt v. Clemson Agr. College of South Carolina, 208 F. Supp. 416 (W.D.S.C. 1962). College desegregation.

Bailey v. Patterson, 206 F. Supp. 67 (S.D. Miss. 1962). Desegregation, interstate and intrastate transportation.

Mapp v. Board of Ed. of City of Chattanooga, Hamilton County, Tennessee, 203 F. Supp. 843 (E.D. Tenn. 1962). School desegregation.

Meredith v. Fair, 202 F. Supp. 224 (S.D. Miss. 1962). University of Mississippi desegregation.

Meredith v. Fair, 199 F. Supp. 754 (S.D. Miss. 1961). University of Mississippi desegregation.

Bailey v. Patterson, 199 F. Supp. 595 (S.D. Miss. 1961). Desegregation, interstate and intrastate transportation.

Brooks v. City of Tallahassee, 202 F. Supp. 56 (N.D. Fla. 1961). Desegregation, transportation, municipal airport restaurant.

Turner v. Randolph, 195 F. Supp. 677 (W.D. Tenn. 1961). Desegregation, Memphis public facilities, public libraries.

Taylor v. Bd. of Ed. of City School Dist. of City of New Rochelle, 195 F. Supp. 231 (S.D.N.Y. 1961). School desegregation.

Turner v. City of Memphis, 199 F. Supp. 585 (W.D. Tenn. 1961). Desegregation, transportation, municipal airport restaurant.

Holmes v. Danner, 191 F. Supp. 394 (M.D. Ga. 1961). University of Georgia desegregation.

Holmes v. Danner, 191 F. Supp. 385 (M.D. Ga. 1960). University of Georgia desegregation.

Calhoun v. Latimer, 188 F. Supp. 412 (N.D. Ga. 1960). Atlanta school desegregation.

Augustus v. Board of Public Instruction of Escambia County, Florida, 185 F. Supp. 450 (N.D. Fla. 1960). Pensacola school desegregation.

Tomkins v. City of Greensboro, North Carolina, 175 F. Supp. 476 (M.D.N.C. 1959). Desegregation, public swimming pool.

Calhoun v. Members of Bd. of Ed., City of Atlanta, Georgia, 188 F. Supp. 401 (N.D. Ga. 1959). School desegregation.

Hunt v. Arnold, 172 F. Supp. 847 (N.D. Ga. 1959). Georgia State College of Business Administration desegregation.

Hawkins v. Board of Control of Florida, 162 F. Supp. 851 (N.D. Fla. 1958). University of Florida desegregation.

Tomkins v. City of Greensboro, North Carolina, 162 F. Supp. 549 (M.D.N.C. 1958). Desegregation, public swimming pool.

Heyward v. Public Housing Administration, 154 F. Supp. 589 (S.D. Ga. 1957). Savannah housing desegregation.

Watts v. Housing Authority of Birmingham Dist., 150 F. Supp. 552 (N.D. Ala. 1956). Housing desegregation.

Heyward v. Public Housing Administration, 135 F. Supp. 217 (S.D. Ga. 1955). Savannah housing desegregation.

Johnson v. Levitt & Sons, Inc., 131 F. Supp. 114 (E.D. Pa. 1955). Levittown housing development discrimination.

Lucy v. Adams, 134 F. Supp. 235 (N.D. Ala. 1955). School discrimination.

Brown v. Baskin, 80 F. Supp. 1017 (E.D.S.C. 1948). White Democratic Party primaries.

Brown v. Baskin, 78 F. Supp. 933 (E.D.S.C. 1948). White Democratic Party primaries.

Harris v. Chappell, 8 R.R.L.R. 1355 (1963). Suit to enjoin Americus insurrection prosecution; Georgia.

Cases before the New York State Commissioner of Education

Matter of School District No. 6, Town of Babylon, 77 State Dept. Repts. 118 (1956).

Matter of School District No. 9, Village of Hempstead, 71 State Dept. Repts. 166 (1950).

Matter of School District No. 1, Village of Hempstead, 71 State Dept. Repts. 133 (1950).

Matter of School District No. 1, Village of Hempstead, 70 State Dept. Repts. 108 (1949).

Matter of W. Scott Davis, et al., 75 State Dept. Repts. 57 (1954).

Matter of Central School District No. 1, Town of Ramapo, 65 State Dept. Repts. 106 (1944).

Notes

Chapter 1. Clarifying and Correcting the Narratives of the Civil Rights Movement

1. *Brown v. Board of Education of Topeka, Kansas*, 347 U.S. 483, 74 S. Ct. 686, 98 L. Ed. 2d 873 (1954).

2. Susan M. Hartmann, *From Margin to Mainstream: American Women and Politics since 1960* (Columbus: Ohio State University, 1989).

3. Zita Allen, *Black Women Leaders of the Civil Rights Movement* (New York: Grolier, 1996); Bernice McNair Barnett, "Invisible Southern Black Women Leaders in the Civil Rights Movement: The Triple Constraints of Gender, Race, and Class," *Gender and Society* 7, no. 2 (June 1993): 162–82; Betty Collier-Thomas and Vincent P. Franklin, eds., *Sisters in the Struggle: African American Women in the Civil Rights Black-Power Movement* (New York: New York University Press, 2001); Vicki L. Crawford, Jacqueline Ann Rouse, and Barbara Woods, eds., *Women in the Civil Rights Movement: Trailblazers and Torchbearers, 1941–1965* (Bloomington: Indiana University Press, 1993); Darlene Clark Hine, Elsa Barkley Brown, and Rosalyn Terborg-Penn, eds., *Black Women in America: An Historical Encyclopedia* (Bloomington: Indiana University Press, 1993); Lynne Olson, *Freedom's Daughters: The Unsung Heroines of the Civil Rights Movement from 1830 to 1970* (New York: Charles Scribner's Sons, 2001); Jo Ann Gibson Robinson, *The Montgomery Bus Boycott and the Women Who Started It: The Memoir of Jo Ann Gibson Robinson*, ed. David J. Garrow (Knoxville: University of Tennessee Press, 1987); Belinda Robnett, "African American Women in the Civil Rights Movement, 1954–1965: Gender, Leadership and Micromobilization," *American Journal of Sociology* 101, no. 6 (May 1996): 1661–93; Belinda Robnett, *How Long? How Long? African American Women in the Struggle for*

Civil Rights (New York: Oxford University Press, 1997); David Halberstam, *The Children* (New York: Random House, 1998).

4. *Plessy v. Ferguson*, 163 U.S. 537, 16 S. Ct. 1138, 41 L. Ed. 25 (1896).

5. See the appendix for a list of Motley's cases.

6. *Hamilton v. State of Alabama*, 368 U.S. 52, 82 S. Ct. 157, 7 L. Ed. 2d 114 (1961); *Turner v. City of Memphis*, 369 U.S. 350, 82 S. Ct. 805, 7 L. Ed. 2d 762 (1962); *Gober v. City of Birmingham*, 373 U.S. 374, 83 S. Ct. 1311, 10 L. Ed. 2d 419 (1963); *Shuttlesworth v. City of Birmingham*, 373 U.S. 262, 83 S. Ct. 1130, 10 L. Ed. 2d 335 (1963); *Bouie v. City of Columbia*, 378 U.S. 347, 84 S. Ct. 1697, 12 L. Ed. 2d 894 (1964); *Barr v. City of Columbia*, 378 U.S. 146, 84 S. Ct. 1734, 12 L. Ed. 2d 766 (1964); *Lupper v. Arkansas*, 377 U.S. 989, 84 S. Ct. 1906, 12 L. Ed. 2d 1043 (1964); *Watson v. City of Memphis*, 373 U.S. 526, 83 S. Ct. 1314, 10 L. Ed. 2d 529 (1963); *Calhoun v. Latimer*, 377 U.S. 263, 84 S. Ct. 1235, 12 L. Ed. 2d 288 (1964); *Swain v. Alabama*, 380 U.S. 202, 85 S. Ct. 824, 13 L. Ed. 2d 759 (1965).

7. *Batson v. Kentucky*, 476 U.S. 79, 106 S. Ct. 1712, 90 L. Ed. 2d 69 (1986). Motley applauded the reversal of Swain in an interview in 2004 and claimed victory in all ten of the cases she argued before the Supreme Court. She stated, "The tenth case I won 20 years later . . . when the court adopted my view that it was a violation of equal protection for prosecutors in criminal cases to use their peremptory challenges to get rid of all of the blacks on a jury panel." Rachel Christmas Derrick, "A Columbian Ahead of Her Time," *Columbia*, Spring 2004.

8. Maya Angelou, telephone interview, June 8, 2011. Angelou, a writer and a civil rights activist who often participated in protests in the South, was personally acquainted with Motley. In our conversation she shared some of her recollections of Motley's experiences in the South and her representation of protesters.

9. Douglas Martin, "Constance Baker Motley, Civil Rights Trailblazer, Dies at 84," *New York Times*, September 29, 2005; Joe Holley, "Constance Motley Dies; Rights Lawyer, Judge," *Washington Post*, September 29, 2995; Drew S. Days III, Remarks at the Funeral Service for the Honorable Constance Baker Motley, US District Judge, New York, October 5, 2005; see also Diane McWhorter, *Carry Me Home: Birmingham, Alabama; The Climactic Battle of the Civil Rights Revolution* (New York: Simon & Schuster, 2001).

10. Howard W. French, "Guiding Wedtech Trial, a Sure Hand," *New York Times*, August 7, 1988.

11. Anne S. Emanuel, "Constance Baker Motley, 1921–2005: Lawyer's Calling Was Civil Rights," *Atlanta Journal-Constitution*, October 10, 2005.

12. Richard Blum, "Constance Juanita Baker Motley," in *The Scribner Encyclopedia of American Lives*, vol. 7, *2003–2005* (New York: Charles Scribner's Sons, 2007), 386; Martin, "Civil Rights Trailblazer"; Holley, "Constance Motley Dies."

Chapter 2. Black Women: On the Front Lines but Not Properly Credited

1. Valeria Harvell, "Social Movement Theory and Black Women's Political Activism," *Proteus* 22, no. 1 (2005):12–13.

2. Ibid., 12–15.

3. Aprele Elliott, "Ella Baker: Free Agent in the Civil Rights Movement," *Journal of Black Studies* 26, no. 5, (May 1996): 593.

4. Crawford et al., *Women in the Civil Rights Movement*, xvii.

5. Francoise N. Hamlin, *Crossroads at Clarksdale The Black Freedom Struggle in the Mississippi Delta after World War II* (Chapel Hill: University of North Carolina Press, 2012), 87–89.

6. Elliott, "Ella Baker," 593.

7. Barnett, "Invisible Southern Black Women," 163–64.

8. Allen, *Black Women Leaders*; Robinson, *Montgomery Bus Boycott*; Robnett, "African American Women"; Belinda Robnett, *How Long?*.

9. Barnett, "Invisible Southern Black Women," 176.

10. Bernard Lafayette Jr., interview, September 18, 2009, Hamden, CT.

11. Halberstam, *Children*, 266, 269–71; "Freedom Riders," *American Experience*, PBS, 2012. The freedom rides were organized by the Congress of Racial Equality to test enforcement of the US Supreme Court decision prohibiting racial segregation in interstate transportation. On May 14, 1960, the riders on the first bus were attacked and viciously beaten by an angry white mob outside Anniston, Alabama; the bus was set on fire and destroyed. When the second bus arrived at the Anniston terminal, the riders on it were attacked and viciously beaten, too. Bernard Lafayette Jr., telephone interview, July 22, 2011; Edythe Scott Bagley, *Desert Rose: The Life and Legacy of Coretta Scott King* (Tuscaloosa: University of Alabama Press, 2012), 156–57.

12. Lafayette interview, September 18, 2009.

13. Barnett, "Invisible Southern Black Women," 176–77; Harvell, "Social Movement Theory," 14.

14. Barnett, "Invisible Southern Black Women," 173–75; Robnett, *How Long?*, 17.

15. Robnett, *How Long?*, 19.

16. Kitty Gellhorn, "The Reminiscences of Judge Constance Baker Motley," oral history, recorded at Columbia University, New York, December 4, 1976, to March 11, 1978, 441.

17. Rhetaugh Graves Dumas, "Dilemmas of Black Females in Leadership," in *The Black Woman*, ed. La Frances Rodgers-Rose (Thousand Oaks, CA: Sage, 1980), 201–4; Barnett, "Invisible Southern Black Women," 170; Anne Standley, "The Role of Black Women in the Civil Rights Movement," in *Women in the Civil Rights Movement: Trailblazers and Torchbearers 1941–1965*, ed. Vicki L. Crawford, Jacqueline Anne Rouse, and Barbara Woods (Bloomington: Indiana University Press, 1993), 183–202.

18. Bettye Collier-Thomas, *Jesus, Jobs, and Justice: African American Women and Religion* (New York: Alfred A. Knopf, 2010).

19. Barnett, "Invisible Southern Black Women," 170.

20. Belinda Robnett, "African American Women," 1664–67, 1669–72.

21. Jacqueline A. Rouse, "We Seek to Know . . . in Order to Speak the Truth: Nurturing the Seeds of Discontent—Septima P. Clark and Participatory Leadership," in *Sisters in the Struggle: African American Women in the Civil Rights Black-Power Movement*, ed. Bettye Collier-Thomas and Vincent P. Franklin (New York: New York University Press, 2001), 116.

22. Herbert Wright, interview, July 20, 2009, Hamden, CT.

23. Hamlin, *Crossroads at Clarksdale*, 87–88.

24. Quoted in Charles Payne, *I've Got the Light of Freedom: The Organizing Tradition and the Mississippi Freedom Struggle* (Berkeley: University of California Press, 1995), 265.

25. Robnett, *How Long?*, 19–26, 113–14.

26. Hamlin, *Crossroads at Clarksdale*, 22–23.

27. Robnett, "African American Women," 1663, 1664, 1679; Robnett, *How Long?*, 16, 17.

28. Barnett, "Invisible Southern Black Women," 165, 168, 169; Christine Greene, *Our Separate Ways: Women and the Black Freedom Movement in Durham, North Carolina* (Chapel Hill: University of North Carolina Press, 2005), 165; Robnett, *How Long?*, 19; Harvell, "Social Movement Theory," 13–17.

29. Barnett, "Invisible Southern Black Women,"168, 169.

30. Constance Baker Motley, "Thurgood Marshall: A Personal Tribute," *Ms.*, September/October 1991.

Chapter 3. Early Life and Preparation to Become a Leader

1. Blum, "Constance Juanita Baker Motley," 384; Martin, "Civil Rights Trailblazer."

2. Constance Baker Motley, *Equal Justice under Law: An Autobiography* (New York: Farrar, Straus & Giroux, 1988), 11, 13; Gellhorn, "Reminiscences," 17–22.

3. Godfrey Hodgson, "Constance Baker Motley: Pioneering Black Woman Lawyer at the Forefront of the Civil Right Struggle in America," *Guardian*, September 30, 2005; Martin, "Civil Rights Trailblazer."

4. Days, Funeral Service Remarks.

5. Gellhorn, "Reminiscences," 30–32.

6. Ibid., 21–22, 35.

7. Ibid., 35, 336.

8. Martin, "Civil Rights Trailblazer."

9. Gellhorn, "Reminiscences," 40, 41, 42.

10. Ibid., 85.

11. Martin, "Civil Rights Trailblazer"; Hodgson, "Pioneering Black Woman Lawyer"; Gellhorn, "Reminiscences," 101, 102.

12. Hodgson, "Pioneering Black Woman Lawyer"; Gellhorn, "Reminiscences," 157.

13. Gellhorn, "Reminiscences," 85–86, 88, 89, 92.

14. Motley, Equal Justice, 41; Blum, "Constance Juanita Baker Motley," 384.

15. Motley, Equal Justice, 41; Days, Funeral Service Remarks; Gellhorn, "Reminiscences," 91–92.

16. Motley, *Equal Justice*, 41.

17. Ibid., 33–34.

18. Louis R. Harlan, ed., *The Booker T. Washington Papers*, vol. 3 (Urbana: University of Illinois Press, 1974), 583–87.

19. David Levering Lewis, *W. E. B. Du Bois: Biography of a Race, 1868–1919* (New York: Henry Holt, 1993), 359.

20. *Missouri ex rel. Gaines v. Canada*, 305 U.S. 337, 59 S. Ct. 233 (1938).

21. Gellhorn, "Reminiscences," 91, 96–97.

22. Motley, Equal Justice, 42 Blum, "Constance Juanita Baker Motley," 384; Martin, "Civil Rights Trailblazer."

23. Blum, "Constance Juanita Baker Motley," 384; Gellhorn, "Reminiscences," 105, 106.

24. Gellhorn, "Reminiscences," 98–100, 106; J. Clay Smith Jr., *Rebels in Law: Voices in History of Black Women Lawyers* (Ann Arbor: University of Michigan Press, 2000), 41.

25. Gellhorn, "Reminiscences," 134.

26. Motley, *Equal Justice*, 42.

27. Motley, Equal Justice, 43; Rachel Christmas Derrick, "A Columbian Ahead of Her Time," *Columbia*, Spring 2004. See also Hodgson, "Pioneering Black Woman Lawyer"; Martin, "Civil Rights Trailblazer"; and Smith, *Rebels in Law*, 41, 42.

28. Motley, Equal Justice, 45; See also Gellhorn, "Reminiscences," 106–7; Smith, *Rebels In Law*, 42.

29. Gellhorn, "Reminiscences," 106–7.

30. Ibid., 107; see also Smith, *Rebels In Law*, 42.

31. Motley, Equal Justice, 45; Blum, "Constance Juanita Baker Motley," 385; "NAACP's Constance Baker Motley Helps Make Legal History: Woman Lawyer behind Atlanta School Victory," *Jet*, June 1959; Martin, "Civil Rights Trailblazer"; Smith, *Rebels In Law*, 42.

32. Gellhorn, "Reminiscences," 109; See also, Motley Equal Justice, 45.

33. Ibid., 110.

34. Gale Thomson, "Constance Baker Motley, 1921–2005," Contemporary Black Biography, http://www.encyclopedia.com.

35. Motley, *Equal Justice*, 47.

36. Gellhorn, "Reminiscences," 111, 112.

37. Motley, *Equal Justice*, 47, 96–97.

38. Martin, "Civil Rights Trailblazer."

39. Florence Wagman Roisman, "An Extraordinary Woman: The Honorable Constance Baker Motley," Indiana Law Review vol. 49:677 (2016), 680, citing Karen Berger Morello, *The Invisible Bar: The Woman Lawyer in America, 1638 to the Present* (New York: Random House, 1986), 159.

40. Martin, "Civil Rights Trailblazer"; Hodgson, "Pioneering Black Woman Lawyer."

41. Gellhorn, "Reminiscences," 114–15.

42. Ibid., 128.

43. Juan Williams, Interview with Joel Motley III, July 13, 2009, New York; Martin, "Civil Rights Trailblazer."

44. Hodgson, "Pioneering Black Woman Lawyer"; Blum, "Constance Juanita Baker Motley," 385.

45. Motley, *Equal Justice*, 55–56.

46. Derrick, "Columbian Ahead of Her Time."

47. Motley, *Equal Justice*, 55–56.

48. Ibid., 56.

49. Ibid., 58–59.

50. Blum, "Constance Juanita Baker Motley," 385; "NAACP's Constance Baker Motley Helps Make Legal History"; Martin, "Civil Rights Trailblazer."

51. Motley, *Equal Justice*, 59.

52. Ibid., 59–60. See also Joe Holley, "Constance Baker Motley Dies"; Elaine R. Jones, "Constance Baker Motley: Defender of Justice," *Crisis*, November/December 2005; and Martin, "Civil Rights Trailblazer."

Chapter 4. Work in the Trenches: The Case-by-Case Implementation of *Brown v. Board of Education*

1. Jane M. Bolin, "Black Women Attorneys in the Legal Profession: A Current Event," *Louisiana Bar Journal* 40, no. 5 (February 1993): 464.

2. Natalie J. Sokoloff, *Black Women and White Women in the Professions: Occupational Segregation by Race and Gender, 1960–1980* (New York: Routledge, 1992), 6.

3. Lin Washington, *Black Judges on Justice: Perspectives from the Bench* (New York: New Press, 1994), 131.

4. Williams, Motley interview.

5. Drew S. Days III, interview, July 15, 2009, New Haven, CT.

6. Hodgson, "Pioneering Black Woman Lawyer." See also Charlayne Hunter-Gault, *In My Place* (New York: Farrar, Straus & Giroux, 1992); and Martin, "Civil Rights Trailblazer."

7. "NAACP's Constance Baker Motley"; Allan Morrison, "Top Woman Civil Rights Lawyer: Securing Rights for Millions, Negro Woman Is One of the World's Most Influential Lawyers," *Ebony*, January 1963; Gellhorn, "Reminiscences," 462; Andrew Young, interview, February 16, 2012, Hamden, CT.

8. Gellhorn, "Reminiscences," 458–60.

9. Bagley, *Desert Rose*, 136. "Unlike state judges," Bagley explained, "federal judges were appointed for life and were not directly subject to the political process. Freed from the need to campaign for reelection, they were somewhat removed from the influence of public sentiment. They also tended to have a worldview that was more cosmopolitan than their counterparts in state court."

10. Motley, "Thurgood Marshall"; see also Gellhorn, "Reminiscences," 458.

11. Morrison, "Top Woman Civil Rights Lawyer."

12. Gellhorn, "Reminiscences," 458.

13. Ibid., 471–72.

14. Derrick Bell, interview, July 13, 2009, New York.

15. Gellhorn, "Reminiscences," 458, 461–62.

16. Ibid., 462; see also *Ebony*, Morrison, "Top Woman Civil Rights Lawyer."

17. Laura Taylor Swain, "Constance Baker Motley, 1921–2005," remarks for Women's History Month, Thurgood Marshall Federal Judiciary Building, Washington, DC, March 29, 2006; Holley, "Constance Baker Motley Dies"; Martin, "Civil Rights Trailblazer"; Motley, *Equal Justice*, 75.

18. Gellhorn, "Reminiscences," 472–73.

19. Motley, *Equal Justice*, 73.

20. Gellhorn, "Reminiscences," 465, 475.

21. Civil Rights Act of 1964, Pub. L. No. 88-352, 78 Stat. 241.

22. Gellhorn, "Reminiscences," 466.

23. Motley, *Equal Justice*, 73–74.

24. Gellhorn, "Reminiscences," 470–71.

25. *Sweatt v. Painter*, 399 U.S. 629, 70 S. Ct. 848; 94 L. Ed. 1114 (1950).

26. Motley, *Equal Justice*, 61, 62.

27. Richard Kluger, *Simple Justice: The History of* Brown v. Board of Education *and Black America's Struggle for Equality* (New York: Vintage Books, 1975), 136.

28. Ibid., 202; see also *Missouri ex rel. Gaines v. Canada*, 305 U.S. 337 (1938).

29. Hamlin, *Crossroads at Clarksdale*, 32.

30. Ibid., 29, 30, 37, 38.

31. Motley, *Equal Justice*, 3–4.

32. Gellhorn, "Reminiscences," 265–66.

33. *Brown v. Board of Education (I)*, 347 U.S. 483 (1954).

34. *Brown v. Board of Education (II)*, 349 U.S. 294, 75 S. Ct. 753, 99 L. Ed. 1083 (1955).

35. Comer Vann Woodward, *The Strange Career of Jim Crow* (New York: Oxford Press, 1955), 147.

36. Ibid.

37. Southern Manifesto on Integration, March 12, 1956, *Congressional Record*, 84th Congress, second session, vol. 102, pt. 4 (Washington, DC: US Government Printing Office, 1956), 4459–60; Juan Williams, *Thurgood Marshall American Revolutionary*, (Times Books Random House, 1998).

38. Woodward, *Strange Career*, 162.

39. Jack Greenberg, interview, July 13, 2009, New York; Herbert Wright, telephone interview, July 17, 2012.

40. Martin, "Civil Rights Trailblazer"; Morrison, "Top Woman Civil Rights Lawyer."

41. Wright interview, July 17, 2012; Juan Williams, *"Thurgood Marshall: American Revolutionary* (New York: Random House, 1998), 248–249; Martin, "Civil Rights Trailblazer."

42. Carolyn Calloway-Thomas and Thurman Garner, "Daisy Bates and the Little Rock School Crisis: Forging the Way," *Journal of Black Studies* 26, no. 5: 616–28; Daisy Bates, *The Long Shadow of Little Rock: A Memoir* (Fayetteville: University of Arkansas Press,1987); Grif Stockley, *Daisy Bates: Civil Rights Crusader from Arkansas* (Jackson: University of Mississippi Press, 2005).

43. "Don't Let Them See You Cry," *Parade*, February 16, 1992; Carlotta Walls LaNier, interview, September 27, 2011, New York.

44. Bagley, *Desert Rose*, 148.

45. Juan Williams, interview with Ernest Green, September 8, 2009, Washington, DC; 2009, LaNier interview, September 27, 2011; Young interview.

46. Williams, Green interview; LaNier interview, September 27, 2011.

47. Williams, Green interview; LaNier interview, September 27, 2011.

48. Carlotta Walls LaNier, e-mail, August 7, 2009.

49. Gellhorn, "Reminiscences," 376.

50. LaNier interview, September 27, 2011.

51. Hamlin, *Crossroads at Clarksdale*, 58.

52. Morrison, "Top Woman Civil Rights Lawyer."

53. Bell interview.

54. Gellhorn, "Reminiscences," 330.

55. Ibid., 281–82.

56. Williams, *Thurgood Marshall*, 248; Wayne Phillips, "University Ousts Miss Lucy Because of Her Charges; Alabama Trustees Permanently Expel Negro Co-ed over Contempt Action; She Flies to New York for Rest," *New York Times*, March 2, 1956.

57. *Lucy v. Adams*, 134 F. Supp. 235 (N.D. Ala. 1955).

58. *Lucy v. Adams*, 350 U.S. 1, 76 S. Ct. 33, 100 L. Ed. 2d 3 (1955).

59. Phillips, "University Ousts Miss Lucy." The Alabama legislature quickly reacted to Lucy's admission. It immediately introduced bills to cut off the state's appropriation for the all-black Tuskegee Institute "should a negro ever be admitted to an all-white college in the state." The Alabama State Senate also unanimously passed a resolution calling on Congress to appropriate funds for blacks in the South to move to the North, the Midwest, and other areas where they were "wanted," "needed," and could be assimilated.

60. Ibid.; *Williams, Thurgood Marshall*, 248–49; Gellhorn, "Reminiscences," 282–83.

61. Williams, *Thurgood Marshall*, 248–49. In the 1980s the university lifted Lucy's expulsion and invited her back to pursue her education. She reenrolled in 1989 and graduated with her daughter in 1992. There were approximately 1,750 black students at the University of Alabama at that time.

62. Gellhorn, "The Reminiscences of Judge Constance Baker Motley," 283–87.

63. Olson, *Freedom's Daughters*, 87–88, 119; Allen, *Black Women Leaders*, 7–8, 56; Williams, *Thurgood Marshall*, 246; Gellhorn, "Reminiscences," 288–89.

64. Bagley, *Desert Rose*, 113–16; Allen, *Black Women Leaders*, 56, 57.

65. Allen, *Black Women Leaders*.

66. Jeanne Theoharis, *The Rebellious Life of Mrs. Rosa Parks* (Boston: Beacon Press, 2013), 54, 80–81, 90; Olson, *Freedom's Daughters*, 111–13; Allen, *Black Women Leaders*, 56.

67. Bernard Lafayette Jr., interview, April 4, 2011, Hamden, CT.

68. Bagley, *Desert Rose*, 114–15; Allen, *Black Women Leaders*, 57; Theoharis, *Rebellious Life*, 52–54, 57–58; Olson, *Freedom's Daughters*, 93.

69. Taylor Branch, *Parting the Waters: America in the King Years, 1954–1963* (New York: Simon & Schuster 1988), 123; Olson, *Freedom's Daughters, 94*.

70. Bagley, *Desert Rose*, 116.

71. Olson, *Freedom's Daughters*, 90–91, 93, 95, 116–19; Theoharis, *Rebellious Life*, 80–82; Allen, *Black Women Leaders*, 71.

72. Williams, *Thurgood Marshall*, 246–49; Wayne Phillips, "Montgomery Negroes Tell Court of Abuse by City's Bus Drivers," *New York Times*, March 22, 1956.

73. Charlene Crowell, "Dr. King and the 1955–56 Montgomery Bus Boycott: A Year-Long Boycott Begins a Life of Peaceful Protest and Service," *Southern Christian Leadership Conference*, Winter 2011; David Garrow, *Bearing the Cross: Martin Luther King, Jr. and the Southern Christian Leadership Conference* (New York: William Morrow, 1986), 51.

74. Crowell, "Dr. King," 27.

75. Phillips, "University Ousts Miss Lucy."

76. *Browder v. Gayle*, 142 F. Supp. 707 (M.D. Ala. 1956).

77. Garrow, *Bearing the Cross*, 90; Olsen, *Freedom's Daughter*, 90–91, 93, 95, 116–19; Theoharis, *Rebellious Life*, 80–82.

78. Bagley, *Desert Rose*, 171. Simultaneously with the crisis surrounding the admission of Hood and Malone to the University of Alabama, Motley was deeply engaged with the representation of Dr. King and the SCLC in Birmingham.

79. Gellhorn, "Reminiscences," 292–94.

80. Williams, *Thurgood Marshall*, 249.

81. Gellhorn, "Reminiscences," 294.

82. Hunter-Gault, *In My Place*; Emanuel, "Lawyer's Calling"; Holley, "Constance Baker Motley Dies." See also "Celebrating Courage: 50th Anniversary of Desegregation at UGA," University of Georgia, http://desegregation.uga.edu/history; *Red and Black* (University of Georgia newspaper), January 9, 1961, http://www.libs.uga.edu/hargrett/archives/integration/graphics/rbextra.jpg; and Steve Osunsami and Maggy Patrick, "University of Georgia Celebrates Desegregation," *World News*, January 14, 2011.

83. Charlayne Hunter-Gault, interview, September 18, 2009, Hamden, CT.

84. Vernon E. Jordan Jr., interview, September 18, 2009, Hamden, CT.

85. "Celebrating Courage"; *Red and Black*; Osunsami and Patrick, "University of Georgia."

86. *Red and Black*.

87. Gellhorn, "Reminiscences," 268.

88. Hunter-Gault interview; Osunsami and Patrick, "University of Georgia"; *Red and Black*.

89. "Celebrating Courage."

90. Gellhorn, "Reminiscences," 270–72.

91. Jordan interview.

92. Ibid.

93. Ibid.

94. Hunter-Gault interview.

95. Gellhorn, "Reminiscences," 273–75.

96. Hunter-Gault interview.

97. Jordan interview.

98. Calvin Trillin, comments, September 18, 2009, Hamden, CT.

99. Ibid.

100. Williams, Motley interview.

101. Hunter-Gault interview.

102. Williams, Motley interview.

103. "Federal Judge Motley Tells How She Keeps 33-Year Marriage Intact," *Jet*, May 24, 1979.

104. James Howard Meredith, *Three Years in Mississippi* (Blooomington: Indiana University Press, 1966); James Meredith and William Doyle, *A Mission from God: A Memoir and Challenge for America* (New York: Simon & Schuster, 2012); Meredith Coleman McGee, *James Meredith: Warrior and the America That Created Him* (Westport, CT: Praeger, 2012).

105. Motley, *Equal Justice*, 162–63.

106. Hamlin, *Crossroads at Clarksdale*, 25–26, 56–57, 95–96, 106, 111–13, 122–24; Lafayette interview, July 22, 2011; Chana Kai Lee, *For Freedom's Sake: The Life of Fannie Lou Hamer* (Athens: University of Georgia Press, 1999), 152; Olson, *Freedom's Daughters*, 98.

107. Williams, *Thurgood Marshall*, 296; Morrison, "Top Woman Civil Rights Lawyer."

108. Gellhorn, "Reminiscences," 302–3.

109. Ibid., 306, Motley, *Equal Justice*, 164.

110. Motley, *Equal Justice*, 162, 163, 170; Branch, *Parting the Waters*, 386, 647; Charles W. Eagles, *The Price of Defiance: James Meredith and the Integregation of Ole Miss* (Chapel Hill: University of North Carolina Press, 2014), 201, 204–5, 207–9, 214, 219, 221–224; Henry Hampton and Steve Fayer, *Voices of Freedom: An Oral History of the Civil Rights Movement from the 1950s through the 1980s* (New York: Bantam Books, 1990), 115–16; Motley, *Equal Justice*, 163–64.

111. Meredith, *Three Years in Mississippi*.

112. Motley, 166, 168–70; *Meredith v. Fair*, 199 F. Supp. 754 (S.D. Miss. 1961); *Meredith v. Fair*, 298 F.2d 696 (5th Cir. 1962).

113. Motley, *Equal Justice*, 172; Branch, *Parting the Waters*, 647–49, 653–59, 664, 668, 670–71; Hampton and Fayer, *Voices of Freedom*, 116; Gellhorn, "Reminiscences," 303–5.

114. Motley, *Equal Justice*, 182; Branch, *Parting the Waters*, 668–70; Hampton and Fayer, *Voices of Freedom*, 116; Gellhorn, "Reminiscences," 302–4; Greenberg interview; Hamlin, *Crossroads at Clarksdale*, 58, 113; "Mississippi Race Riots over Black Student," BBC, October 1, 1962, http://news.bbc.co.uk/onthisday/hi/dates/stories/october/1/newsid_2538169. stm); "3,000 Troops Put Down Mississippi Rioting and Seize 200 As Negro Attends Classes; Ex Gen. Walker Is Held for Insurrection," *New York Times*, October 2, 1962.

115. "Mississippi Race Riots"; Branch, *Parting the Waters*, 657–59, 667–68, 670; Motley, *Equal Justice*, 182; Hampton and Fayer, *Voices of Freedom*, 116.

116. Holley, "Constance Baker Motley Dies"; Derrick, "Columbian Ahead of Her Time."

117. Bell interview.

118. Blum, "Constance Juanita Baker Motley," 384–86.

119. "Mississippi Race Riots"; Branch, *Parting the Waters*, 671.

120. Gellhorn, "Reminiscences," 377.

121. Motley, "The Legacy of *Brown v. Board of Education*," 1994.

122. Ibid.

123. Gellhorn, "Reminiscences," 380–81.

124. Ibid., 313.

125. Hamlin, *Crossroads at Clarksdale*, 34.

126. Ibid., 22.

127. Gellhorn, "Reminiscences," 378–79.

128. Hamlin, *Crossroads at Clarksdale*, 9, 13, 25–27, 47–48, 56–57, 95–97, 110, 111, 112–113, 122–124.

129. Ibid., 36, 46, 47.

130. Gellhorn, "Reminiscences," 307–9.

131. *Stell v. Savannah-Chatham County Bd. of Ed.*, 220 F. Supp. 667 (S.D. Ga. 1963).

132. *Stell v. Savannah-Chatham County Bd. of Ed.*, 318 F.2d 425 (5th Cir. 1963).

133. *Bush v. Orleans Parish School Board*, 308 F.2d 491 (5th Cir. 1962).

134. Gellhorn, "Reminiscences," 503.

135. Wright interview, July 17, 2012; Bell interview.

136. Bell interview.

137. Gellhorn, "Reminiscences," 414.

138. Motley, *Equal Justice*, 181.

139. Gellhorn, "Reminiscences," 493–95; Williams, Motley interview.

140. Gellhorn, "Reminiscences," 493–95.

141. Motley, *Equal Justice*, 180.

142. Gellhorn, "Reminiscences," 417.

143. Ibid., 251, 526–27.

144. Ibid., 262.

145. Ibid., 416–17.

146. Ibid., 264–65.

147. "Congressman John Lewis Remembers Constance Motley," US House of Representatives, December 2, 2005, http://www.house.gov/johnlewis/05pressrelease/pr093005.html.

Chapter 5. Representing Protesters:
Mass Demonstrations, Marches, Sit-Ins, and Freedom Rides

1. *Rice v. Elmore*, 165 F.2d 387 (4th Cir. 1947).

2. Gellhorn, "Reminiscences," 333–34.

3. Wyatt Tee Walker, letter, April 17, 2009.

4. Holley, "Constance Baker Motley Dies"; "Attorneys-at-Law: Constance Baker Motley," *Black Enterprise*, August 1977.

5. Martin Luther King to Constance Baker Motley, February 10, 1964, and Motley to King, February 12, 1964, Sophia Smith Collection, Smith College, Northhampton, MA, http://www.smith.edu/libraries/libs/ssc/agents/motley.html.

6. Gellhorn, "Reminiscences," 553.

7. Young interview.

8. Bernard Lafayette Jr., interview, February 16, 2012, Hamden, CT.

9. Ibid.; Young interview; Wright interview, July 17, 2012.

10. "Press Statement regarding Crusade for Citizenship," October 5, 1957, King Center, http://www.thekingcenter.org/archive/document/press-statement-regarding-crusade-citizenship.

11. Martin Luther King to Vice President Nixon, August 30, 1957, King Center, http://www.thekingcenter.org/archive/document/letter-mlk-vicepresident-nixon-0#.

12. Lafayette interview, April 4, 2011.

13. Ibid.

14. Ibid.

15. Ibid.

16. Ibid.

17. Ibid.

18. Motley, *Equal Justice*, 138.

19. Gellhorn, "Reminiscences," 423–24; see also Motley, *Equal Justice*, 138.

20. Gellhorn, "Reminiscences," 480; see also Motley, *Equal Justice*, 139.

21. Motley, *Equal Justice*, 139.

22. Ibid., 140; Gellhorn, "Reminiscences," 423–28.

23. Gellhorn, "Reminiscences," 424; Motley, *Equal Justice*, 139.

24. Motley, *Equal Justice*, 140.

25. Ibid,, 140; see also Gellhorn, "Reminiscences," 423–28.

26. Young interview; Lafayette interview, April 4, 2011; Wright interview, July 17, 2012.

27. Gellhorn, "Reminiscences," 429.

28. Bagley, *Desert Rose*, 161; Lafayette interview, April 4, 2011.

29. Lafayette interview, April 4, 2011.

30. Ibid.

31. Bagley, *Desert Rose*, 166–67; Lafayette interview, April 4, 2011.

32. Bagley, *Desert Rose*, 167; see also McWhorter, , 410–11.

33. "The Birmingham Truce Agreement, May 10, 1963," in *The Eyes on the Prize Civil Rights Reader: Documents, Speeches, and Firsthand Accounts from the Black Freedom Struggle*, ed. Clayborne Carson, David J. Garrow, Gerald Gill, Vincent Harding, and Darlene Clark Hine, (New York: Penguin, 1991), 159.

34. Motley, *Equal Justice*, 135; Bagley, *Desert Rose*, 171.

35. Motley, *Equal Justice*, 135.

36. Ibid., 135–36; McWhorter, *Carry Me Home*, 444; Calvin Woods, interview, August 11, 2014, Birmingham, AL.

37. Gellhorn, "Reminiscences," 429, 430.

38. Motley, *Equal Justice*, 136.

39. Gellhorn, "Reminiscences," 431.

40. Ibid., 430, 431; Motley, *Equal Justice*, 136.

41. Motley, *Equal Justice*, 135–36.

42. Ibid., 136; Emanuel, "Lawyer's Calling"; Gelhorn, "Reminiscences," 431–36.

43. McWhorter, *Carry Me Home*, 450–51.

44. Emanuel, "Lawyer's Calling."

45. Woods interview; Motley, *Equal Justice*, 136.

46. Woods interview; McWhorter, *Carry Me Home*, 450–51; Motley, *Equal Justice*, 136.

47. Woods interview; Emanuel, "Lawyer's Calling"; Gellhorn, "Reminiscences," 431–36; McWhorter, *Carry Me Home*, 450–51; Motley, *Equal Justice*, 136–37.

48. Motley, *Equal Justice*, 136, 137.

49. Gellhorn, "Reminiscences," 433–34.

50. Ibid., 435–36.

51. Woods interview; Young interview; Williams, Motley interview.

52. Gellhorn, "Reminiscences," 435–36.

53. Martin, "Civil Rights Trailblazer."

54. Williams, Motley interview.

55. Gellhorn, "Reminiscences," 437.

56. Ibid., 438.

57. Days interview.

58. Wright interview, July 20, 2009.

59. Motley, *Equal Justice*, 199.

60. Gellhorn, "Reminiscences," 532.

61. Halberstam, *Children*, 3–10; Lafayette interview, April 4, 2011.

62. Gellhorn, "Reminiscences," 534.

63. Ibid., 534–35.

64. Lafayette interview, April 4, 2011.

65. Gellhorn, "Reminiscences," 531–32.

66. *Hamm v. City of Rock Hill, Lupper v. State of Arkansas*, 379 U.S. 306, 85 S. Ct. 384, 13 L. Ed. 2d 300 (1964).

67. Wright interview, July 20, 2009.

68. Hamlin, *Crossroads at Clarksdale*, 75.

69. Wright interview, July 20, 2009.

70. Martin, "Civil Rights Trailblazer"; Lynn Huntley "The Measure of Greatness: Thoughts about the Honorable Constance Baker Motley," unpublished paper, December 5, 2005.

71. Lee, *For Freedom's Sake*, 152.

72. LaNier interview, September 27, 2011; Olson, Freedom's Daughters, 122..

73. Lafayette interview, April 4,, 2011.

74. Charles J. Ogletree, interview, July 13, 2009, New York.

75. Juan Williams, Interview with William T. Coleman Jr., September 8, 2009, Washington, DC.

76. Wright interview, July 20, 2009.

77. Wright interview, July 17, 2012.

78. Wright interview, July 20, 2009.

79. Days interview.

80. Williams, Motley interview.

81. Hamlin, *Crossroads at Clarksdale*, 112.

Chapter 6. Desegregating America, Case by Case, in the Supreme Court

1. James Nabrit, e-mail, April 16, 2009.

2. Ibid.

3. *Hamilton v. State of Alabama*, 368 U.S. 52 (1961).

4. Gellhorn, "Reminiscences," 511, 513–514.

5. *Turner v. City of Memphis*, 369 U.S. 350 (1962).

6. *Gober v. City of Birmingham*, 373 U.S. 374 (1963).

7. *Shuttlesworth v. City of Birmingham*, 373 U.S. 262 (1963).

8. Motley, *Equal Justice*, 196.

9. *Watson v. City of Memphis*, 373 U.S. 526 (1963).

10. *Calhoun v. Latimer*, 377 U.S. 263 (1964).

11. Motley, *Equal Justice*, 197–98.

12. *Bouie v. City of Columbia*, 378 U.S. 347 (1964).

13. *Barr v. City of Columbia*, 378 U.S. 146 (1964).

14. *Hamm v. City of Rock Hill*, 377 U.S. 988, 84 S. Ct. 1902, 12 L. Ed. 2d 1042 (1964); *Lupper v. Arkansas*, 377 U.S. 989 (1964); *Hamm v. City of Rock Hill, Lupper v. State of Arkansas*, 379 U.S. 306 (1964).

15. Motley, *Equal Justice*, 199.

16. *Swain v. Alabama*, 380 U.S. 202 (1965).

17. Gellhorn, "Reminiscences," 543–44.

18. *Batson v. Kentucky*, 476 U.S. 79 (1986).

19. Derrick, "Columbian Ahead of Her Time."

20. Motley, *Equal Justice*, 201–2

21. Days interview.

Chapter 7. The Transition from Activist Movement Lawyer

1. Williams, Motley interview.

2. Motley, *Equal Justice*, 151.

3. Greenberg interview.

4. Motley, *Equal Justice*, 151.

5. Ibid.

6. Hartmann, *From Margin to Mainstream*, 22.

7. *Ibid.*, 24.

8. Douglas Schoen, comments, September 18, 2009, Hamden, CT.

9. Motley, *Equal Justice*, 204–5.

10. Ibid., 206.

11. French, "Guiding Wedtech Trial."

12. Schoen comments; see also Motley, *Equal Justice*, 207.

13. Schoen comments.

14. Judge Constance Bake Motley Papers, Sophia Smith Collection, Smith College, Northhampton, MA, http://www. smith. edu/libraries/libs/ssc/agents/motley. html.

15. Schoen comments.

16. Days, Funeral Service Remarks.

17. Swain, "Constance Baker Motley, 1921–2005."

18. Motley, *Equal Justice*, 212.

19. Lin Washington, Lin, *Black Judges on Justice*, 127.

20. Ibid., 129.

21. Swain, "Constance Baker Motley, 1921–2005."

22. French, "Guiding Wedtech Trial"; see also Hodgson, "Pioneering Black Woman Lawyer."

23. Williams, Motley interview.

24. Smith, *Rebels in Law*, 44.

25. *Motley, Equal Justice*, 221.

26. Ibid.

27. Ibid., 224.

28. Swain, "Constance Baker Motley, 1921–2005."

29. Ibid.

30. Ibid.

31. James Farmer, comments, September 18, 2009, Hamden, CT.

32. Swain, "Constance Baker Motley, 1921–2005."

33. Laura Taylor Swain, comments, July 13, 2009, New York.

34. Farmer comments.

35. French, "Guiding Wedtech Trial."

36. Swain, "Constance Baker Motley, 1921–2005."

37. Farmer comments.

38. Swain, "Constance Baker Motley, 1921–2005."

39. Farmer comments.

40. Farmer comments.

41. Days interview.

42. Farmer comments.

43. Ibid.

44. Swain, "Constance Baker Motley, 1921–2005."

45. Ibid.

46. Farmer comments.

47. Ibid.

48. Ibid.

49. William Forbath, comments, September 18, 2009, Hamden, CT.

50. Swain, "Constance Baker Motley, 1921–2005."

51. Williams, Motley interview.

52. Swain, "Constance Baker Motley, 1921–2005."

53. Ibid.

54. Ibid.

55. Ibid.

56. *Sostre v. Rockefeller*, 312 F. Supp. 863 (S.D.N.Y. 1970).

57. Gellhorn, "Reminiscences," 13–15.

58. Ibid., 13.

59. Ibid.,15, 18.

60. Derrick, "Columbian Ahead of Her Time."

61. Forbath comments.

62. *Letke v. Bouie Kuhn*, 461 F. Supp. 86 (S.D.N.Y. 1978).

63. Motley, *Equal Justice*, 226.

64. Swain, "Constance Baker Motley, 1921–2005."

65. John Brittain, e-mail, April 30, 2009. "Perhaps her low and soft demeanor belied her brilliance and inner tenacity to lead people to overlook her tremendous contributions. To further speculate, her proud West Indian and Caribbean ancestry from the small island of Nevis may have played a role in her modest ways."

66. "President Clinton Awards Presidential Citizens Medals," National Archives, clinton5.nara. gov/WH/new/html/Mon_Jan_8_141714_2001. html.

67. Swain, "Constance Baker Motley, 1921–2005."

68. Swain comments.

Conclusion

1. Huntley e-mail.

2. Gellhorn, "Reminiscences," 363–64.

Bibliography

ARCHIVE

Sophia Smith Collection, Smith College, Northhampton, MA, http://www.smith.edu/libraries/libs/ssc/agents/motley.html.

Martin Luther King Jr.'s correspondence with Constance Baker Motley
James H. Meredith's correspondence with Constance Baker Motley
Judge Constance Baker Motley Papers

BOOKS

Allen, Zita. *Black Women Leaders of the Civil Rights Movement*. New York: Grolier, 1996.

Bagley, Edythe Scott. *Desert Rose: The Life and Legacy of Coretta Scott King*. Tuscaloosa: University of Alabama Press, 2012.

Barrett, Russell H. *Integration at Ole Miss*. Chicago: Quadrangle Books, 1965.

Bates, Daisy. *The Long Shadow of Little Rock: A Memoir*. Fayetteville: University of Arkansas Press, 1987.

"The Birmingham Truce Agreement, May 10, 1963." In *The Eyes on the Prize Civil Rights Reader: Documents, Speeches, and Firsthand Accounts from the Black Freedom Struggle*, ed. Clayborne Carson, David J. Garrow, Gerald Gill, Vincent Harding, and Darlene Clark Hine, 159. New York: Penguin, 1991.

Blum, Richard. "Constance Juanita Baker Motley." In *The Scribner Encyclopedia of American Lives*. Vol. 7, *2003–2005*, 384–386. New York: Charles Scribner's Sons, 2007.

Branch, Taylor. *Parting the Waters: America in the King Years, 1954–1963*. New York: Simon & Schuster, 1988.

Brenner, Marie. *Great Dames: What I Learned from Older Women*. New York: Crown, 2000.

Collier-Thomas, Bettye. *Jesus, Jobs, and Justice*: African American Women and Religion. New York: Alfred A. Knopf, 2010.

Collier-Thomas, Bettye, and Vincent P. Franklin, eds. *Sisters in the Struggle: African American Women in the Civil Rights Black-Power Movement*. New York: New York University Press, 2001.

Crawford, Vicki L., Jacqueline Ann Rouse, and Barbara Woods, eds. *Women in the Civil Rights Movement: Trailblazers and Torchbearers, 1941–1965*. Bloomington: Indiana University Press, 1993.

Crowe, Chris. *Up Close: Thurgood Marshall*. New York: Penguin, 2008.

Du Bois, W. E. B. *The Souls of Black Folk*. Cambridge, UK: Cambridge University Press, 1903.

Dumas, Rhetaugh Graves. "Dilemmas of Black Females in Leadership." In *The Black Woman*, edited by La Frances Rodgers-Rose, 201–4. Thousand Oaks, CA: Sage, 1980.

Eagles, Charles, W. *The Price of Defiance: James Meredith and the Integration of Ole Miss*. Chapel Hill: University of North Carolina Press, 2014.

Epstein, Cynthia Fuchs. *Women in the Law*. New York: Basic Books, 1981.

Fleming, Cynthia. "Black Women and Black Power: The Case of Ruby Doris Smith Robinson and the Student Nonviolent Coordinating Committee." In *Sisters in the Struggle: African American Women in the Civil Rights Black-Power Movement*, edited by Bettye Collier-Thomas and Vincent P. Franklin, 197–213. New York: New York University Press, 2001.

———. *Soon We Will Not Cry: The Liberation of Ruby Doris Smith Robinson*. Lanham, MD: Rowman & Littlefield, 1998.

Garrow, David. *Bearing the Cross: Martin Luther King, Jr., and the Southern Christian Leadership Conference*. New York: William Morrow, 1986.

Grant, Joanne. *Ella Baker: Freedom Bound*. Hoboken, NJ: John Wiley & Sons, 1998.

Greenberg, Jack. *Crusaders in the Courts: Legal Battles of the Civil Rights Movement*. New York: Twelve Tables Press, 2004.

Greene, Christine. *Our Separate Ways: Women and the Black Freedom Movement in Durham, North Carolina*. Chapel Hill: University of North Carolina Press, 2005.

Halberstam, David. *The Children*. New York: Random House, 1998.

Hamlin, Francoise N. *Crossroads at Clarksdale: The Black Freedom Struggle in the Mississippi Delta after World War II*. Chapel Hill: University of North Carolina Press, 2012.

Hampton, Henry, and Steve Fayer. *An Oral History of the Civil Rights Movement from the 1950s through the 1980s*. New York: Bantom Books, 1990.

Harlan, Louis R., ed. *The Booker T. Washington Papers*. Vol. 3. Urbana: University of Illinois Press, 1974.

Hartmann, Susan M. *From Margin to Mainstream: American Women and Politics since 1960*. Columbus: Ohio State University, 1989.

Hine, Darlene Clark, Elsa Barkley Brown, and Rosalyn Terborg-Penn, eds. *Black Women in America: An Historical Encyclopedia*. Bloomington: Indiana University Press, 1993.

Hunter-Gault, Charlayne. *In My Place*. New York: Farrar, Straus & Giroux, 1992.

———. *To the Mountaintop: My Journey through the Civil Rights Movement*. New York: Roaring Book Press, 2012.

Kirk, John. "Daisy Bates, the National Association for the Advancement of Colored People, and the 1957 Little Rock School Crisis: A Gendered Perspective." In *Gender and the Civil Rights Movement*, edited by Peter J. Ling and Sharon Monteith, 17–40 (New York: Garland, 1999).

Kluger, Richard. *Simple Justice: The History of* Brown v. Board of Education *and Black America's Struggle for Equality*. New York: Vintage Books, 1975.

LaNier, Carlotta Walls. *A Mighty Long Way: My Journey to Justice at Little Rock Central High School*. New York: One World/Ballantine, 2009.

Lanker, Brian. *I Dream a World: Portraits of Black Women Who Changed America*. New York: Stewart, Tabori & Change, 1989.

Lee, Chana Kai. *For Freedom's Sake: The Life of Fannie Lou Hamer*. Athens: University of Georgia Press, 1999.

Lewis, David Levering. *W. E. B. Du Bois: Biography of a Race, 1868–1919*. New York: Henry Holt, 1993.

Ling, Peter J., and Sharon Monteith, eds. *Gender and the Civil Rights Movement*. New York: Garland, 1999.

McGee, Meredith Coleman. *James Meredith: Warrior and the America That Created Him*. Westport, CT: Praeger, 2012.

McWhorter, Diane. *Carry Me Home: Birmingham, Alabama; The Climactic Battle of the Civil Rights Revolution*. New York: Simon & Schuster, 2001.

Meredith, James Howard. *Three Years in Mississippi*. Bloomington: Indiana University Press, 1966.

Meredith, James, and William Doyle. *A Mission from God: A Memoir and Challenge for America*. New York: Simon & Schuster, 2012.

Mills, Kay. *This Little Light of Mine: The Life of Fannie Lou Hamer*. New York: E. P. Dutton, 1993.

Morello, Karen Berger. *The Invisible Bar: The Woman Lawyer in America, 1638 to the Present*. New York: Random House, 1986.

Motley, Constance Baker. *Equal Justice under Law: An Autobiography*. New York: Farrar, Straus & Giroux, 1988.

Mullins, Lisa. *Diane Nash: Fire of the Civil Rights Movement*. Miami, FL: Barnhardt & Ashe, 2007.

Olson, Lynne. *Freedom's Daughters: The Unsung Heroines of the Civil Rights Movement from 1830 to 1970*. New York: Charles Scribner's Sons, 2001.

Payne, Charles. *I've Got the Light of Freedom: The Organizing Tradition and the Mississippi Freedom Struggle*. Berkeley: University of California Press, 1995.

Pratt, Robert A. *We Shall Not Be Moved: The Desegregation of the University of Georgia*. Athens: University of Georgia Press, 2002.

Ransby, Barbara. *Ella Baker and the Black Freedom Movement: A Radical Democratic Vision*. Chapel Hill: University of North Carolina Press, 2003.

Robinson, Jo Ann Gibson. *The Montgomery Bus Boycott and the Women Who Started It: The Memoir of Jo Ann Gibson Robinson*. Edited by David J. Garrow. Knoxville: University of Tennessee Press, 1987.

Robnett, Belinda. *How Long? How Long? African American Women in the Struggle for Civil Rights*. New York: Oxford University Press, 1997.

———. "Women in the Student Nonviolent Coordinating Committee: Ideology, Organizational Structure, and Leadership." In *Gender and the Civil Rights Movement*, edited by Peter J. Ling and Sharon Monteith, 131–69. New York: Garland, 1999.

Rouse, Jacqueline A. "We Seek to Know . . . in Order to Speak the Truth: Nurturing the Seeds of Discontent—Septima P. Clark and Participatory Leadership." In *Sisters in the Struggle: African American Women in the Civil Rights Black-Power Movement*, edited by Bettye Collier-Thomas and Vincent P. Franklin, 96–119. New York: New York University Press, 2001.

Sartain, Lee. *Invisible Activists: Women of the Louisiana NAACP and the Struggle for Civil Rights, 1915–1945*. Baton Rouge: Louisiana State University, 2007.

Smith, J. Clay Jr. *Rebels in Law: Voices in History of Black Women Lawyers*. Ann Arbor: University of Michigan Press, 2000.

Sokoloff, Natalie J. *Black Women and White Women in the Professions: Occupational Segregation by Race and Gender, 1960–1980*. New York: Routledge, 1992.

Standley, Anne. "The Role of Black Women in the Civil Rights Movement." In *Women in the Civil Rights Movement: Trailblazers and Torchbearers, 1941–1965*, edited by Vicki L. Crawford, Jacqueline Anne Rouse, and Barbara Woods, 183–202. Bloomington: Indiana University Press, 1993.

Stockley, Grif. *Daisy Bates: Civil Rights Crusader from Arkansas*. Jackson: University of Mississippi Press, 2005.

Theoharis, Jeanne. *The Rebellious Life of Mrs. Rosa Parks*. Boston: Beacon Press, 2013.

Washington, Booker T. *The Booker T. Washington Papers*. Vol. 3. Urbana: University of Illinois Press, 1974.

Washington, Lin. *Black Judges on Justice: Perspectives from the Bench*. New York: New Press, 1994.

Williams, Juan. *Eyes on the Prize: America's Civil Rights Years, 1954–1965*. New York: Penguin Press, 1988.

———. *Thurgood Marshall: American Revolutionary*. New York: Random House, 1998.

Woodward, Comer Vann. *The Strange Career of Jim Crow*. New York: Oxford Press, 1955.

COURT CASES

Barr v. City of Columbia, 378 U.S. 146, 84 S. Ct. 1734, 12 L. Ed. 2d 766 (1964).

Batson v. Kentucky, 476 U.S. 79, 106 S. Ct. 1712, 90 L. Ed. 2d 69 (1986).

Bouie v. City of Columbia, 378 U.S. 347, 84 S. Ct. 1697, 12 L. Ed. 2d 894 (1964).

Browder v. Gayle, 142 F. Supp. 707 (M.D. Ala. 1956).

Brown v. Board of Education of Topeka, Kansas, 347, 74 S. Ct. 686, 98 L. Ed. 2d 873 U.S. 483 (1954). (Also called *Brown I*.)

Brown v. Board of Education (II), 349 U.S. 294, 75 S. Ct. 753, 99 L. Ed. 1083 (1955).

Bush v. Orleans Parish School Board, 308 F.2d 491 (5th Cir. 1962).

Calhoun v. Latimer, 377 U.S. 263, 84 S. Ct. 1235, 12 L. Ed. 2d 288 (1964).

Gober v. City of Birmingham, 373 U.S. 374, 83 S. Ct. 1311, 10 L. Ed. 2d 419 (1963).

Hamilton v. State of Alabama, 368 U.S. 52, 82 S. Ct. 157, 7 L. Ed. 2d 114 (1961).

Hamm v. City of Rock Hill, 377 U.S. 988, 84 S. Ct. 1902, 12 L. Ed. 2d 1042 (1964).

Hamm v. City of Rock Hill, Lupper v. State of Arkansas, 379 U.S. 306, 85 S. Ct. 384, 13 L. Ed. 2d 300 (1964).

Letke v. Bouie Kuhn, 461 F. Supp. 86 (S.D.N.Y. 1978).

Lucy v. Adams, 350 U.S. 1, 76 S. Ct. 33, 100 L. Ed. 2d 3 (1955).

Lucy v. Adams, 134 F. Supp. 235 (N.D. Ala. 1955).

Lupper v. Arkansas, 377 U.S. 989, 84 S. Ct. 1906, 12 L. Ed. 2d 1043 (1964).

Meredith v. Fair, 298 F.2d 696 (5th Cir. 1962).

Meredith v. Fair, 199 F. Supp. 754 (S.D. Miss. 1961).

Missouri ex rel. Gaines v. Canada, 305 U.S. 337, 59 S. Ct. 233 (1938).

Plessy v. Ferguson, 163 U.S. 537, 16 S. Ct. 1138, 41 L. Ed. 25 (1896).

Rice v. Elmore, 165 F.2d 387 (4th Cir., S.C. 1947).

Shuttlesworth v. City of Birmingham, 373 U.S. 262, 83 S. Ct. 1130, 10 L. Ed. 2d 335 (1963).

Sostre v. Rockefeller, 312 F. Supp. 863 (S.D.N.Y. 1970).

Stell v. Savannah-Chatham County Bd. of Ed., 318 F.2d 425 (5th Cir. 1963).

Stell v. Savannah-Chatham County Bd. of Ed., 220 F. Supp. 667 (S.D. Ga. 1963).

Swain v. Alabama, 380 U.S. 202, 85 S. Ct. 824, 13 L. Ed. 2d 759 (1965).

Sweatt v. Painter, 399 U.S. 629, 70 S. Ct. 848; 94 L. Ed. 1114 (1950).

Turner v. City of Memphis, 369 U.S. 350, 82 S. Ct. 805, 7 L. Ed. 2d 762 (1962).

Watson v. City of Memphis, 373 U.S. 526, 83 S. Ct. 1314, 10 L. Ed. 2d 529 (1963).

LEGISLATION

Civil Rights Act of 1964, Pub. L. No. 88-352, 78 Stat. 241.

DOCUMENTARY

"Freedom Riders," *American Experience*, PBS, 2012.

ONLINE SOURCES

"Celebrating Courage: 50th Anniversary of Desegregation at UGA," University of Georgia, http://desegregation.uga.edu/history.

"Congressman John Lewis Remembers Constance Motley," US House of Representatives, December 2, 2005, http://www.house.gov/johnlewis/05pressreleases/pr093005.html.

Martin Luther King to Vice President Richard Nixon, August 30, 1957, King Center, http://www.thekingcenter.org/archive/document/letter-mlk-vicepresident-nixon-0#.

"Mississippi Race Riots over Black Student," BBC, October 1, 1962, http://news.bbc.co .uk/onthisday/hi/dates/stories/october/1/newsid_2538169.stm)

"Motley, Constance Baker (1921–2005)," National Women's History Project, http://www .nwhp.org/whm/motley_bio.php.

"President Clinton Awards Presidential Citizens Medals," National Archives, clinton5. nara.gov/WH/new/html/Mon_Jan_8_141714_2001.html.

"Press Statement Regarding Crusade for Citizenship," October 5, 1957, King Center, http://www.thekingcenter.org/archive/document/press-statement-regarding-crusade-citizenship.

Thomson, Gale. "Constance Baker Motley, 1921–2005." Contemporary Black Biography, http://www.encyclopedia.com.

PERIODICALS

Alpin, Charles L. "Jo Ann Gibson Robinson: The Woman Who Initiated the Montgomery Bus Boycott." *Southern Christian Leadership Conference*, Winter 2011.

"Attorneys-at-Law: Constance Baker Motley." *Black Enterprise*, August 1977.

Barnett, Bernice McNair. "Invisible Southern Black Women Leaders in the Civil Rights Movement: The Triple Constraints of Gender, Race, and Class." *Gender and Society* 7, no. 2 (June 1993): 162–82.

Berg, Allison. "Trauma and Testimony in Black Women's Civil Rights Memoirs: The Montgomery Bus Boycott and the Women Who Started It, Warriors Don't Cry, and From the Mississippi Delta." *Journal of Women's History* 21, no. 3 (Fall 2009): 84–107.

Bolin, Jane M. "Black Women Attorneys in the Legal Profession: A Current Event." *Louisiana Bar Journal* 40, no. 5 (February 1993): 464.

Calloway-Thomas, Carolyn, and Thurman Garner. "Daisy Bates and the Little Rock School Crisis: Forging the Way." *Journal of Black Studies* 26, no. 5: 616–28.

"Constance Baker Motley." *New York Times*, October 3, 2005.

Crawford, Vicki L. "In Memoriam: Coretta Scott King and the Struggle for Civil and Human Rights; An Enduring Legacy." *Journal of African American History* 92, no. 1 (Winter 2007): 106–117.

Crowell, Charlene. "Dr. King and the 1955–56 Montgomery Bus Boycott: A Year-Long Boycott Begins a Life of Peaceful Protest and Service." *Southern Christian Leadership Conference*, Winter 2011.

Derrick, Rachel Christmas. "A Columbian Ahead of Her Time." *Columbia*, Spring 2004.

"Don't Let Them See You Cry." *Parade*, February 16, 1992.

Elliott, Aprele. "Ella Baker: Free Agent in the Civil Rights Movement." *Journal of Black Studies* 26, no. 5 (May 1996): 593–603.

Emanuel, Anne S. "Constance Baker Motley, 1921–2005: Lawyer's Calling Was Civil Rights." *Atlanta Journal-Constitution*, October 10, 2005.

"Federal Judge Motley Tells How She Keeps 33-Year Marriage Intact." *Jet*, May 24, 1979.

French, Howard. "Guiding Wedtech Trial, a Sure Hand." *New York Times*, August 7, 1988.

Hamlet, Janice. "Fannie Lou Hamer: The Unquenchable Spirit of the Civil Rights Movement." *Journal of Black Studies* 26 (1996): 560–76.

Harvell, Valeria. "Social Movement Theory and Black Women's Political Activism." *Proteus* 22, no. 1 (2005):12–18.

Hodgson, Godfrey. "Constance Baker Motley: Pioneering Black Woman Lawyer at the Forefront of the Civil Rights Struggle in America." *Guardian,* September 30, 2005.

Holley, Joe. "Constance Baker Motley Dies; Rights Lawyer, Judge. *Washington Post*, September 29, 2005.

Jones, Elaine R. "Constance Baker Motley: Defender of Justice." *Crisis*, November/December 2005.

Martin, Douglas. "Constance Baker Motley, Civil Rights Trailblazer, Dies at 84." *New York Times*, September 29, 2005.

Morrison, Allan. "Top Woman Civil Rights Lawyer: Securing Rights for Millions, Negro Woman Is One of the World's Most Influential Lawyers." *Ebony*, January 1963.

Motley, Constance Baker. "Desegregation and Education." *Mississippi Law Journal* 58 (Fall 1988): 241.

———. "James Meredith in Perspective." *Crisis*, January 1963.

———. "Massive Resistance: America's Second Civil War." *Arkansas Law Journal* 41 (1988): 130.

———. "My Personal Debt to Thurgood Marshall." *Yale Law Journal* 101, no. 1 (October 1991): 19–24.

———. "Some Recollections of My Career." *Law and Inequality* 6 (1988): 35–40.

———. "Thurgood Marshall: A Personal Tribute." *Ms.*, September/October 1991.

"NAACP's Constance Baker Motley Helps Make Legal History: Woman Lawyer behind Atlanta School Victory." *Jet*, June 1959.

"Negro Women in Politics." *Ebony*, August 1966.

Osunsami, Steve, and Maggy Patrick. "University of Georgia Celebrates Desegregation." *World News*, January 14, 2011.

Phillips, Wayne. "Montgomery Negroes Tell Court of Abuse by City's Bus Drivers." *New York Times*, March 22, 1956.

———. "University Ousts Miss Lucy Because of Her Charges; Alabama Trustees Permanently Expel Negro Co-ed over Contempt Action; She Flies to New York for Rest." *New York Times*, March 2, 1956.

Quindlen, Anna. "A Case History: Judge Motley versus Life." *New York Times*, Aug. 25, 1977.

Red and Black (University of Georgia newspaper), January 9, 1961. http://www.libs.uga.edu/hargrett/archives/integration/graphics/rbextra.jpg.

Robnett, Belinda. "African American Women in the Civil Rights Movement, 1954–1965: Gender, Leadership, and Micromobilization." *American Journal of Sociology* 101, no. 6 (May 1996): 1661–93.

Roisman, Florence Wagman, "An Extraordinary Woman: The Honorable Constance Baker Motley." Indiana Law Review vol. 49:677 (2016)

"3,000 Troops Put Down Mississippi Rioting and Seize 200 As Negro Attends Classes; Ex Gen. Walker Is Held for Insurrection." *New York Times*, October 2, 1962.

Wickham, Wayne. "Four Lionesses Put Their Imprint on History." *USA Today*, November 23, 2005.

UNPUBLISHED SOURCES

Days, Drew S. III. Remarks at the Funeral Service for the Honorable Constance Baker Motley, US District Judge, New York, October 5, 2005.

Gellhorn, Kitty. "The Reminiscences of Judge Constance Baker Motley." Oral history, recorded at Columbia University, New York, December 4, 1976, to March 11, 1978.

Huntley, Lynn. "The Measure of Greatness: Thoughts about the Honorable Constance Baker Motley," December 5, 2005.

Motley, Constance Baker. "The Brown Case Transformed American Society."

———. "The Legacy of *Brown v. Board of Education*," 1994.

———. Remarks at the Annual Meeting of the Association of Black Women Attorneys, New York, September 30, 2003.

———. Remarks on the Occasion of Hanging a Portrait in the Constance Baker Motley Jury Assembly Room, New York, May 14, 2003.

Peacock, Jardana. "Geographies of Mentorship: Black Women and the Civil Rights Movement; A Case Study of Septima Clark and Ella Baker." Master's thesis, University of Louisville, Kentucky, 2008.

Swain, Laura Taylor. "Constance Baker Motley, 1921–2005." Remarks for Women's History Month, Thurgood Marshall Federal Judiciary Building, Washington, DC, March 29, 2006.

VanDelinder, Jean. "Interview with Constance Baker Motley: *Brown v. Board of Education of Topeka* Oral History Project." Kansas State Historical Society, October 6, 1992.

Williams, Juan. Interview with William T. Coleman Jr., September 8, 2009, Washington, DC.

———. Interview with Ernest Green, September 8, 2009, Washington, DC.

———. Interview with Joel Motley III, July 13, 2009, New York.

Comments, Interviews, and Personal Correspondence with the Author

Maya Angelou, June 8, 2011, telephone.

Derrick Bell, July 13, 2009, New York.

John Brittain, April 30, 2009, e-mail.

Bill Clinton, August 3, 2011, recorded comments.

Drew S. Days III, July 15, 2009, New Haven, CT.

James Farmer, September 18, 2009, Hamden, CT.

William Forbath, September 18, 2009, Hamden, CT.

Jack Greenberg, July 13, 2009, New York.

Charlayne Hunter-Gault, September 18, 2009, Hamden, CT.

Lynn Huntley, April 9, 2009, e-mail.

Elaine Jones, September 18, 2009, Hamden, CT.

Vernon E. Jordan Jr., September 18, 2009, Hamden, CT.

Bernard Lafayette Jr., July 22, 2011, telephone; September 18, 2009, April 4, 2011, and February 16, 2012, Hamden, CT.

Carlotta Walls LaNier, August 7, 2009, e-mail; September 27, 2011, New York; September 28, 2011, Hamden, CT.

James Nabrit, April 16, 2009, e-mail.

Charles J. Ogletree, July 13, 2009, New York.

Douglas Schoen, September 18, 2009, Hamden, CT.

Laura Taylor Swain, July, 13, 2009, New York.

Calvin Trillin, September 18, 2009, Hamden, CT.

Wyatt Tee Walker, April 17, 2009, letter.
Juan Williams, September 18, 2009, Hamden, CT.
Calvin Woods, August 11, 2014, Birmingham, AL.
Herbert Wright, July 20, 2009, Hamden, CT; July 17, 2012, telephone.
Andrew Young, February 16, 2012, Hamden, CT.

Index